M000208597

SECRET
CALIFORNIA

A Guide to the Weird, Wonderful, and Obscure

Ruth Carlson

Copyright © 2021, Reedy Press, LLC
All rights reserved.

Reedy Press
PO Box 5131
St. Louis, MO 63139
www.reedypress.com

No part of this publication may be reproduced or transmitted in any form or by any means, electronic or mechanical, including photocopy, recording, or any information storage and retrieval system, without permission in writing from the publisher. Permissions may be sought directly from Reedy Press at the above mailing address or via our website at www.reedypress.com.

Library of Congress Control Number: 2021935145
ISBN: 9781681063317

Design by Jill Halpin

Unless otherwise indicated, all photos are courtesy of the author or in the public domain. Back cover photo by Linda Benyahia.

We (the publisher and the author) have done our best to provide the most accurate information available when this book was completed. However, we make no warranty, guarantee, or promise about the accuracy, completeness, or currency of the information provided, and we expressly disclaim all warranties, express or implied. Please note that attractions, company names, addresses, websites, and phone numbers are subject to change or closure, and this is outside of our control. We are not responsible for any loss, damage, injury, or inconvenience that may occur due to the use of this book. When exploring new destinations, please do your homework before you go. You are responsible for your own safety and health when using this book.

Printed in the United States of America
21 22 23 24 25   5 4 3 2 1

To my nine wonderful siblings, Susan, Bill, Paul, Debbie, Bobbie, David, Cathy, Carrie, and especially Jane, everyone's second mother. Mom always said someday we'd be grateful for our large family!

CONTENTS

INTRODUCTION

Legend has it the name California comes from a 16th-century Spanish romance novel about an island full of gold ruled by Queen Califia. The Golden State, home to Hollywood, the Gold Country, Silicon Valley, and that City by the Bay, has always been a place that seems more magical than real.

Since the beginning, this state has been home to dreamers, explorers, and artists who thrive in its natural beauty and embrace its freedom and open attitude. Because of them, California has the first neon art museum, a frog monument, a puppet theater, gardens honoring immigrant workers, architecture out of a sci-fi novel, and water temples.

From Angels Camp to ZZYZX, author Ruth Carlson has uncovered quirky spots that will surprise even locals. This is not a book for tourists but rather for travelers who want to immerse themselves in the culture, history, and quirkiness of California.

Tourists visit attractions and check them off their list while travelers seek out the weird, wonderful, and obscure. Secret California introduces travelers to a woman who created the only perfume museum in the US, a man in the middle of the desert who's writing the history of the world in granite, an artist who makes robot art out of trash, a woman who saved Chicken Boy (aka the Los Angeles Statue of Liberty), and a collector of muffler men, you'll have to read the book to find out what they are.

Secret California also educates travelers on the state's history: why Sacramento has an underground city, why Jack London was such a prolific writer, (hint: he loved his Beauty Ranch), who promised Utopia in Tiburon, and how an underground resort happened in Fresno.

This is the reason California is so interesting, the reason we live here, and the reason people come from all over the world to visit.

If you've read this far, you're a traveler, so visit the Room of the Dons at the Mark Hopkins Hotel to see the murals of Queen Califia and begin your magical journey of California.

BEACHWARE

What defunct pottery factory is still dishing out place settings?

In California, there's a beach for everyone. . . surfers, swimmers, sunbathers, volleyball players, kayakers, and nudists. But there's only one beach just for ceramic lovers.

Visitors gaze at the ground here instead of out to sea, conducting amateur archaeological digs through shards of vintage pottery. It's a quiet beach; the only sounds are the melodic sound of boots crunching layers of blue, pink, white, and green plates accompanied by bird calls and the occasional squeal of delight when a digger discovers a rare intact inscribed plate.

It's called TEPCO beach, short for Technical Porcelain and Chinaware Company, and it was a dumping ground for defective pottery. As shocking as this sounds today, environmental laws were lax when TEPCO started using the beach, and the area's population was considerably smaller.

Potter John Pagliero, an Italian immigrant, created TEPCO in the early 1900s and ran it with his family until it closed in the '60s. At one point TEPCO was the largest employer in El Cerrito, and their heavy-duty ceramics were popular with consumers, the Army, the Navy, and restaurants. Today ceramic collectors covet the personalized restaurant dinnerware: mugs for the Doggie Diner chain, tiki tumblers for Trader Vic's, and plates adorned with jumping frogs for an Angels Camp restaurant for instance. Don't despair if

PORCELAIN BEACH

WHAT: TEPCO Beach

WHERE: Behind Costco, 4801 Central Ave., Richmond

COST: Free

PRO TIP: Visit at low tide for the best selection of pottery.

Left: *Too many people looking for ceramics on the beach miss the beautiful view along the Point Isabel Shoreline in Richmond.*

Right: *A beach covered in ceramics is crunchy, but if you're willing to look you might find some free treasures!*

you don't find an intact piece of pottery. The broken shards are perfect for mosaics.

In addition to the treasured restaurant settings, many search for tiny Buddha heads that curiously have nothing to do with TEPCO. For an art project, Casey O'Connor, a Sierra College professor, threw hundreds of these Buddhas into various waterways, and many washed up on TEPCO Beach on the southern end of Point Isabel.

The Richmond Museum of History and Culture, housed in a Carnegie library built in 1910, has more details about the impact of the TEPCO factory in the community.

FELICITATIONS

Why are there monuments in the middle of the desert?

New York, Paris, London, as much as you think you're the center of the universe, bad news. That honor belongs to Felicity, California. It's not the financial, fashion, or cultural epicenter of the world, but France and Imperial County, California, have declared it the world's midpoint.

How this happened is entirely due to one charismatic and persistent man, Jacques-André Istel, who convinced these governments it was in their best interest to choose this random spot as the center of the earth.

A true renaissance man, he grew up in Paris, started the first parachute company in the United States, wrote a children's book (about Felicity), and is continually building the Museum of History in Granite. If you have problems with the accuracy of the words written on triangles in the sand, take it up with the mayor. Istel was unanimously elected mayor ad infinitum by the town's two residents—Istel and his wife, Felicia. He jokes that he named the town after his wife because it was cheaper than buying her a fur coat.

Felicity has a replica of a chapel in Brittany, an outdoor staircase from the Eiffel Tower, and granite triangles etched with the history of the world. There's also a maze where you can have the name of your deceased loved

HISTORY CARVED IN STONE

WHAT: The Official Center of the World

WHERE: Felicity

COST: $8 for a tour, $5 on your own

PRO TIP: If you are taking a ride share from Felicity, CA to the nearest airport, Yuma in Arizona, you won't be able to use Uber or Lyft (drivers can't cross state lines). Instead call Desert Drivers (928-613-2500).

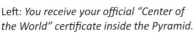

Left: *You receive your official "Center of the World" certificate inside the Pyramid.*

Right: *You can pay to have your loved ones name engraved on the maze.*

Inset: *A strange sign to see in the desert.*

one inscribed for a fee. Take a tour, and when you enter the Pyramid you'll receive a certificate of your visit to the center of the world.

Istel, who discovered this land while based at Camp Pendleton as a Marine during the Korean War, says planning the next chapter of his outdoor manuscript keeps him out of mischief.

Tour the nearby Yuma Territorial Prison, now a state historic park along the Colorado River. Inmates here had to build their own cells!

DIVE BAR DIORAMAS

When is a mini-bar not a bar?

Remember the country song "I'm Gonna Hire a Wino to Decorate Our Home"? If renovating your home to resemble a tavern is not your aesthetic, how about adding a tiny replica of a dive bar to your fireplace mantle instead?

Sentimental patrons of local watering holes keep Santa Barbara artist Michael E. Long busy making intricate dioramas. His attention to detail includes crooked artworks on the bar walls, beer cans, neon signs, and even cigarette burns.

It started with his favorite dive bar, Elsie's Tavern. Elsie's has no sign or street number, but locals know it offers Pop-Tarts, Pac-Man, pool, and pop for adults. Since Long re-created this bar in miniature, he's been inundated with requests for models of quirky neighborhood haunts.

His assemblages immortalize a Santa Barbara most tourists never see, including the Pickle Room, the Mercury Lounge, La Bamba, and the Mecca Sports bar. Long's version of Jimmy's Oriental Gardens, one of the last remnants of Santa Barbara's Chinatown, was purchased by a woman making

ONE FOR THE ROAD

WHAT: Dive bar art

WHERE: The Rondo, 202 W Canon Perdido, Santa Barbara

COST: Free to look; prices vary

PRO TIP: Make an appointment to visit. As the sign says, the Rondo is open . . . sometimes.

Find your inner artist along the UC Santa Barbara Labyrinth Trail. A tranquil spot made of granite and river rock, it leads to nowhere and everywhere your mind takes you.

Left: *Artist Michael Long in front of the Rondo Gallery which is not a Voodoo Church!*

Top right: *Most tourists don't know about the locals hangout, Elsie's Tavern.*

Bottom right: *Jimmy's Oriental Gardens lives on through Long's artwork. Photo courtesy of Michael Long*

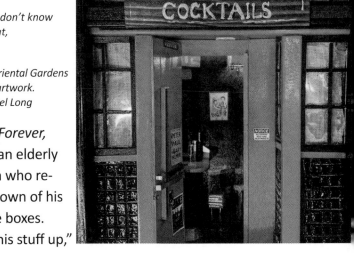

the documentary *Forever, Chinatown* about an elderly San Francisco man who re-creates the Chinatown of his youth in miniature boxes. "You can't make this stuff up," chuckles Long.

A former teacher and bartender, he says these jobs prepared him well for his current career, and that his technique is "making art from junk that I find."

Long works out of The Rondo Art Gallery, whose motto is "not a Voodoo Church," and yes, he's recreated the studio in a diorama.

CHEESE WAR

Who invented Jack Cheese?

Monterey Jack grates on the nerves of Pacifica residents, who claim Monterey doesn't know jack. Just ask Kathleen Manning, an antiquarian bookseller, cookbook collector, and former president of the Pacifica Historical Society (PHS). When she came across the 1937 book *Eating Around San Francisco*, she was thrilled to find a Pacifica restaurant, Mori Point Inn, listed in the category "Best Eateries" alongside the prestigious Palace Hotel and Fisherman's Grotto.

The cookbook raved about the cheese created by the Italian-born Mori family, whose inn and restaurant dated back to the 1870s. When one of his employees left, he stole the cheese recipe and took it with him to his new job at Jack Ranch in Monterey . . . hence the name.

With this information, Pacifica has reclaimed its historic cheese legacy, and Manning says, "We have a lot of fun with it." The city hired a fromager to make a Pacifica Jack cheese, which is sold at the Pacifica Coastside Museum. "It's a very simple recipe, with no preservatives," says Manning, who has a new moniker, "the cheesy lady."

If Pacifica Jack inspires you to be cheesier, stop by the restaurant with the searchlights on the Pacific. Nick's Restaurant in the city's Rockaway Beach area has a retro horseshoe lounge where you can sip a martini with your prawn cocktail before dancing to Frank Sinatra songs.

Left: *Monterey and Pacifica share many things, including fog, the ocean, and kayakers, but only one can claim they invented Jack cheese!*

Right: *Even if Pacifica never gets to claim rightful ownership of their cheese, they take comfort in their ruggedly beautiful surroundings.*

Inset: *Pacifica is serious about re-claiming its cheesy heritage.*

SHREDDING IN PACIFICA

WHAT: Pacifica Jack cheese

WHERE: Pacifica Coastside Museum, 1850 Francisco Blvd., Pacifica

COST: $8 a pound; $10 includes a towel with the phrase "If you don't know Pacifica, you don't know Jack."

PRO TIP: A Grape in the Fog and other local restaurants feature Pacifica Jack dishes on their menus.

Locals also compete in an annual contest for the best Pacifica Jack cheese recipe, and one year Monterey protesters showed up. Locals were quite upset, says Manning, until they realized the picketers were a joke. Mori family members have attended the competition and are thrilled their legacy lives on, according to Manning. (The Mori Point Inn burned down in the 1960s.)

ROBOLIGHTS

What do robots, aliens, and Santa have in common?

On a suburban lawn in Palm Springs, palm trees surround Santa riding his sleigh past a shark; a merry-go-round; and colossal fuchsia, cobalt blue, and neon-yellow robots.

This sculpture garden on acid is courtesy of artist Kenny Irwin Jr., who "takes people's old junk and creates works of art—stuff that would have ended up in a landfill," he says. Washing machines, mannequins, bicycles, vacuum cleaners, and even toilets are reincarnated at "Robolights." Irwin's fascination with robots dates back to age nine, when he built his first one from wood. He's also partial to creating Christmas displays and creatures from outer space.

"I believe alien life exists," he says. "There are things beyond our comprehension, and it transcends through my art. It is about exploration, and it uplifts and inspires."

JUNK YARD

WHAT: A suburban yard filled with junk converted to quirky large-scale art.

WHERE: 1077 E Granvia Valmonte, Palm Springs

COST: Free

PRO TIP: To schedule a private tour for only $10, text 1-760-774-0318

At the downtown Henry Frank Arcade Building, you can look through a telescope and see the profile of Abraham Lincoln on Mount San Jacinto.

Left: *Carousel rides co-exist with robots in this Palm Springs art exhibit.*

Right: *Robolights may be the most unusual yard in the country.*

Inset: *Beware of land sharks in the Robolights exhibit!*

He describes this curious mix of large-scale sculptures as "lighthearted, whimsical art . . . that combines things you wouldn't necessarily think of. It's a why not in a why world, and I say why not."

Irwin staged an elaborate Christmas light display until it outgrew the neighborhood—73,000 attended over five weeks. Now he's searching for a larger outdoor space to stage his annual holiday event. "What I'd really like to do is build an amusement park," he adds.

For now, this exhibition is free for anyone who drives or walks by the house. "It gives people great pleasure. I love to see people smile and laugh," says Irwin.

HAND OF THE LAND

Where does Napa's most famous artist create his masterpieces?

Bicycling along the rolling backroads of Napa, you pass lush vineyards, stone walls, tasting rooms, and a giant orange hand holding a white ball . . . wait, what?!

This perfect Insta moment is located outside artist Gordon Huether's studio. *Hand of the Land*, symbolizing a winery worker holding a grape, is surrounded by enormous neon-colored metal and acrylic sculptures swaying in the wind.

Inside the cavernous workshop you'll spot Huether in the air teetering on a tightrope . . . or rather a full-size replica of the self-proclaimed "bad boy" of the art world. He boasts that he never went to art school. Instead, his unorthodox education began with helping his father create window displays for a Napa department store. After the shop closed, a friend gave Huether some of the mannequins, which he covered in a mosaic of shattered glass.

THERE'S MORE TO NAPA THAN WINE

WHAT: Gordon Huether Studio + Gallery

WHERE: 1821 Monticello Rd., Napa

COST: Free

PRO TIP: Along the Art Walk, stop in at the Brown Estate, the only Black-owned winery in Napa and the first in the nation.

Epicureans should visit the Chuck Williams Culinary Arts Museum, where they'll find decorative rolling pins, butter molds, a duck press, and tureens shaped like rabbits.

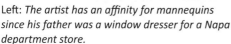

Left: *The artist has an affinity for mannequins since his father was a window dresser for a Napa department store.*

Right: *Heuther's sculpture* Hand of the Land *is an homage to those who work in the vineyards.*

Inset: *A sculpture of the sculptor walking a tight rope.*

In the studio you can watch artists creating Huether's next inspiration and see replicas of his large-scale art installations, including a three-dimensional tarantula hanging out in a Morgan Hill garage, a futuristic "canyon" the size of a football field installed at the Salt Lake City airport, and statues of Robert and Margrit Mondavi drinking wine on the roof of the Culinary Institute of America at Copia.

If you're lucky, the artist himself will be available to show you around. He's a Napa native, and much of downtown is sprinkled with his creations, including a 9/11 memorial garden constructed using Twin Towers beams gifted to Napa firefighters.

FAMOUS FROGS

Do you know a good trainer . . . for amphibians?

When Samuel Clemens, a.k.a. Mark Twain, published "The Celebrated Jumping Frog of Calaveras County," he became a media darling and was finally able to indulge his expensive tastes. He would be tickled to know that the amphibians he made famous are now pampered as well.

Can you blame the Calaveras County frogs for being divas? In the spa underneath the stage constructed for the annual Frog Jump Jubilee, their legs are massaged and the water is cool. In fact, locals say many frogs purposely perform lackluster jumps so they can return to the frog spa.

Winners are immortalized in brass on the Frog Hop of Fame in downtown Angels Camp, just like the Hollywood Walk of Fame down south. Contestants have been featured on the Netflix show *We Are the Champions*, and Brown University has studied their muscle power.

Since 1928, every third weekend in May frog jockeys from around the world, including many families who pass down secret coaching tips through generations, gather in this

AMPHIBIAN ATHLETES

WHAT: Frog Hop of Fame

WHERE: Main Street, Angels Camp

COST: Free

PRO TIP: If you don't happen to own a frog, no problem. During the Frog Jump Jubilee you can rent one for $5 and try your luck on the smaller Lily Pad stage.

The Angels Camp Museum has great exhibits on both Mark Twain and the frog jumping contest.

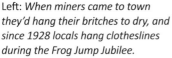

Left: *When miners came to town they'd hang their britches to dry, and since 1928 locals hang clotheslines during the Frog Jump Jubilee.*

Right: *Blowing, dancing, yelling, coaches will try anything. Photo courtesy of Jeff White*

Inset: *Winners are immortalized on the Frog Hop of Fame in downtown Angels Camp.*

gold rush town to compete for the coveted trophy. During the Frog Jump Jubilee, the town's population explodes from 3,000 to 50,000. Pros bring their own frogs they've scouted in secret places. After placing their frog on the starting lily pad, contestants try anything to get it hopping: dancing, singing, whistling, yelling, and sometimes even blowing on its butt. But they can't touch it.

The world record is held by Rosie the Ribiter. If your frog beats Rosie, who jumped 21 feet, 5-3/4 inches in 1986, you get $5,000 and a brass plaque on the Frog Hop of Fame.

The frogs are protected by the Fish and Wildlife Service, so they're released into the wild after the festivities, even if they're reluctant to leave the spa.

MYSTERY SPOT

Can you trust your sixth sense?

Balls roll uphill, people walk on walls, and compasses go crazy. It all happens at the Mystery Spot in Santa Cruz. But the biggest mystery of all is how our eyes fool us.

A tilting cabin on a steep hillside in the middle of a redwood forest, it became a roadside attraction for new motorists in 1940 after surveyors discovered it defied the laws of gravity.

It's old-fashioned corny fun. Young guides practice their stand-up comedy acts while engaging the audience in various demonstrations: pushing, pulling, standing, and often feeling dizzy afterward. Weight hangs from the ceiling vertically, but the tilt of the cabin makes it appear to be suspended at an angle. Visitors pushing the weights one way find it more difficult than pushing them the other way. It's not a magical defiance of gravity; it's a mismatch between expectations and actual weight, wrote the late Bruce Bridgeman, a University of California, Santa Cruz, psychology professor who studied the Mystery Spot illusions.

Bridgeman said the phenomenon is proprioception, often called the sixth sense. Your eyes see one thing without a horizon to compare it with, and your mind can't accept that

---

The grounds are littered with Banana Slugs, the University of California, Santa Cruz mascot. Students adopted this lowly mascot as a rebuke to traditional University athletic programs and you can stock up on banana slug souvenirs at the UCSC bookstore.

TAKE A LEAP OF FAITH

WHAT: Mystery Spot

WHERE: 465 Mystery Spot Rd., Santa Cruz

COST: $8 plus $5 parking

PRO TIP: Take a hike and enjoy a picnic under a redwood canopy.

Top left: *Some say there is no exit from the Mystery spot.*

Top right: *It's no mystery why people love the Santa Cruz boardwalk.*

Bottom: *Everyone gets a free Mystery Spot bumper sticker-not everyone covers their cars in them.*

you are on flat ground, even after the guides pull out a level. It's the same problem pilots of small planes can have confusing the sea with the sky. "We think of our perceptions as being pretty much accurate, but they seldom are," Bridgeman wrote. "People are notoriously inaccurate when they attempt to estimate things like distance and the slope of a hill. We're wrong, but we're right enough to get us there," said Bridgeman.

Alternatively, some say aliens are to blame.

When you leave you get a free neon-yellow Mystery Spot bumper sticker; you'll spot others just like it all over town.

IT'S COMPLICATED

When is technology a curse?

With the complicated name Reuben Garrett Lucius Goldberg and a degree in engineering from the University of California, Berkeley, maybe it's no surprise Rube Goldberg is famous for creating cartoons of convoluted machines to perform simple tasks.

A San Francisco native, Goldberg quickly abandoned engineering for the artistic life. The San Francisco Chronicle hired him to draw for the sports page, but New York was where ambitious young men went in those days. His cartoons of crazy, complicated mechanical solutions for simple tasks were a big hit in the *New York Evening Mail* and the *New York Sun*. The machines used pulleys, levers, birds, and rockets for problems such as getting the last olive out of a jar or using a napkin.

Goldberg is the only person listed as an adjective in the dictionary. As early as 1931, the Merriam-Webster Dictionary defined "Rube Goldberg" as "accomplishing by complex means what seemingly could be done simply."

For all the laughs his cartoons generated they also conveyed an underlying message: technology designed to simplify your life may actually make it more complicated. His art also addressed current events, his atomic bomb illustration won a Pulitzer Prize.

Despite his rise to stardom in New York, Goldberg never forgot San Francisco. He commissioned a mixed-use building at Gough and Oak streets with businesses downstairs and two apartments upstairs: one for his father, the deputy sheriff of San

---

The Bancroft Library at UC Berkeley has the majority of Goldberg's work, but it's difficult to access, so you might require a Rube Goldberg machine to see the collection.

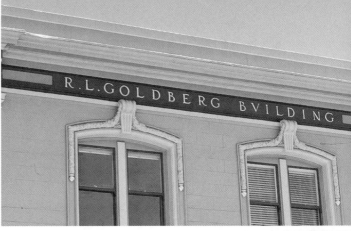

R.L. GOLDBERG BVILDING

Top left: *After finding fame and fortune in NY, Goldberg bought a building in SF he visited often.*

Top right: *Goldberg bought this mixed-use building so his father could live upstairs, he could visit from New York, and the businesses below would bring in income.*

Bottom left: *Self-scrubbing brush: A classic Rube Goldberg contraption.*

Bottom right: *Goldberg saw the future of home entertainment. Photos courtesy of Rube Goldberg Foundation*

HISTORIC HIJINKS

WHAT: Rube Goldberg building

WHERE: 198 Gough St., San Francisco

COST: Free

PRO TIP: You can see an artist's rendering of Goldberg in Coit Tower. Halfway up the staircase, he's the man in the very tall hat.

Francisco, and one for him to visit. This historic landmark has "R. L. Goldberg" inscribed on the frieze.

Every year his granddaughter Jennifer George holds a Rube Goldberg Machine Contest, where students compete to see who can dream up the zaniest contraption.

SAN FRANCISCO'S SECRET WEAPON

What might save San Francisco after a nuclear attack?

Once upon a time a San Francisco boy walked by a castle every day and dreamed of being king. This magical place survived earthquakes, Prohibition, and threats of nuclear war, all due to a secret weapon—plain old water.

Albion Castle was built around 1870 by an Englishman named John Hamlin Burnell. He took advantage of the city's bustling shipyards, using ballast stones and wood from abandoned ships to build his home. Underneath the castle was a fresh spring, just the thing he needed to brew beer for the 800 saloons in town.

The Albion Porter and Ale Brewery was very popular until Prohibition. But all was not lost. Thanks to the underground spring, Albion switched from making beer to selling water, which came in handy when the 1906 earthquake damaged pipes supplying H_2O.

Decades later, the castle was almost bulldozed, but once again the springs saved the day. It was the height of the Cold War, and the *San Francisco Chronicle* successfully argued that it might be the city's only non-contaminated source of fresh water if there was a nuclear attack.

Learn more about the city's shipbuilding past at the new Crane Cove Park linking Mission Bay and Dogpatch. The name comes from two historic cranes workers named Nick and Nora, after the main characters in the Thin Man movies from the 1930s and '40s.

Left: *Albion Castle overlooks the once-thriving shipbuilding area of San Francisco.*

Right: *The Albion brewery was successful because of the underground water supply.*

Over the years a series of artists moved in, adding medieval touches, sculptures in the gardens, and a throne in the bathroom. When it came up for sale again in 2012, that little boy, now a San Francisco police lieutenant, fulfilled his dream. Bill Gilbert never moved in, but his family gathers there for celebrations, and he rents it for retreats, often to tech companies.

THE POWER OF WATER

WHAT: Albion Castle

WHERE: 881 Innes Ave., San Francisco

COST: Free to walk outside the castle

PRO TIP: The castle is isolated, so be aware of your surroundings.

CRAFTY CHURCH

What building inspired the Arts and Crafts movement?

The who's who of San Francisco in 1895, along with some ethereal spirits, had a part in building the Swedenborgian Church, the city's only house of worship with national historic landmark status. Located in tony Pacific Heights, a few blocks from "Billionaires' Row," this modest building is an early example of the Arts and Crafts movement.

Swedenborgian Church is based on the theological writings of an 18th-century Swede, Emanuel Swedenborg. A Renaissance man, he dabbled in anatomy, geology, philosophy, astronomy, religion, and even clairvoyance. According to one legend, the queen of Sweden instructed Swedenborg to ask her deceased brother a question. When Swedenborg gave the queen the answer, she went pale because it was something no one but her brother could know.

His ideas caught on in SF, and in 1895 pastor Joseph Worcester built the Swedenborgian Church with help from his influential friends, naturalist John Muir, architect Bernard Maybeck, artist William Keith, and philanthropist Phoebe Hearst, mother of William Randolph Hearst. Robert Frost was baptized in the clamshell-shaped font donated by Hearst, and many say the church's teachings influenced his poems.

Nature was the overarching theme of the chapel, so instead of the typical grand entrance parishioners walk by a garden filled with trees from around the world. Madrone beams, personally selected by Worcester from the Santa Cruz forest, hold up the

RELAXED RELIGION

WHAT: Swedenborgian Church

WHERE: 2107 Lyon St., San Francisco

COST: Free

PRO TIP: Pack a lunch and enjoy a serene break from the frantic city in the gardens.

Left: *Reverend Junchol Lee says the church is a popular spot for weddings.*

Right: *This is one of few churches in San Francisco with a working fireplace.*

Inset: *Bernard Maybeck had a role in designing the church, an early example of the Arts and Crafts movement.*

ceiling and adorn William Keith's paintings of the four seasons. Swedenborgian feels like a cozy cabin rather than a church, with handmade maple chairs instead of pews and a working wood fireplace. Sunday services are open to the public.

The home used in the *Full House* TV show and it's remake is located nearby at 1709 Broderick. The Victorian has changed paint colors and owners many times since then, but tourists still like to grab selfies here.

PAPER TREASURES

What's the best beach read?

Among the swanky shops and wine bars in downtown Santa Barbara hides the world's largest private collection of important original documents, the Karpeles Manuscript Library.

Walking inside this cool, white stucco building, you'll encounter a dinosaur (a replica of one from *Jurassic Park*), historic models of clipper ships, a copy of the globe used by Christopher Columbus, and vibrant modern paintings. Despite the name, the library is not restricted to manuscripts.

Priceless papers include early sketches of Walt Disney cartoons, a 350-year-old Torah written on deerskin, Richard Nixon's resignation speech, Albert Einstein's handwritten $E=mc^2$ formula, and Noah Webster's *American Dictionary of the English Language*.

Founded by David Karpeles, who made his fortune investing in real estate, the museum is dedicated to preserving written works of literature, science, religion, government, and

A MILLION MANUSCRIPTS

WHAT: Karpeles Manuscript Library

WHERE: 21 W Anapamu St., Santa Barbara

COST: Free

PRO TIP: Manuscripts may not sound like something children would enjoy but the museum is a big hit with young people.

Find more antique manuscripts at the Book Den in downtown Santa Barbara. This 80-year-old bookstore stocks new, used and out of print books on topics ranging from art and literature to the sciences.

Left: *Take a break from the beach to visit the Karpeles Manuscript Library.*

Top and bottom right: *Although it's a manuscript museum the owner doesn't let that stop him from collecting whatever catches his fancy, including replicas of dinosaurs and schooners.*

Inset: *Hiding among downtown restaurants and shops is reportedly the largest manuscript museum in the world.*

art. After opening the Santa Barbara museum in 1986 he opened 16 other manuscript libraries across the country, and displays rotate between locations.

Permanent treasures in Santa Barbara include an original stone copy of the Declaration of Independence, the computer guidance system used on the first Apollo flight to the moon, and handwritten musical scores by Bach and Mozart.

On Sunday afternoons there are lectures in the 100-seat auditorium, and in the summer the patio is taken over by young chess players.

A MANY-SIDED STORY

What classy dames saved a wacky house?

Octagon houses were all the rage in the 1850s thanks to a book by Orson Squire Fowler. *The Octagon House: A Home for All* championed eight-sided homes because all the windows provided the maximum amount of sunlight. William McElroy and his wife, Harriet, believed the hype and built an octagonal house at Gough and Union in the Cow Hollow district of San Francisco. After William died, Harriet took in boarders, including writer Daniel O'Connell, a co-founder of the Bohemian Club.

By the 1950s the house needed major renovations, and the current owner, Pacific Gas and Electric, (PG&E), was more than happy to donate it to the National Society of the Colonial Dames of America, who needed a place to house their antiques. During the restoration workers discovered McElroy's time capsule, a tin box containing newspaper clippings about the country's civil unrest, a photo of his family, and a letter "to the future." The missive remarked upon San Francisco's population explosion due to the gold rush and joked that he and his wife were a very good-looking old couple. They were in their 40s!

Today the McElroy Octagon house is a museum for colonial-era decorative arts as well as histroic documents related to the

Keep walking to Russian Hill to see another octagon house on Green Street's Paris block. These homes survived the fires following the 1906 earthquake because many residents refused to leave.

Octagon Houses were all the rage in the late 1800s.

COLONIAL COUP

WHAT: McElroy Octagon House

WHERE: 2645 Gough St., San Francisco

COST: Free, donations accepted

PRO TIP: The museum has limited hours, so call ahead to make sure it is open.

founding of the United States. A painting of George Washington, pewter dinnerware, needlepoint samplers, and ceramics are on display. The antique furniture collection includes a "birdcage" table that spins around like a lazy Susan, a traveling desk, and a cherrywood clock inset with Birdseye maple.

FAST FOOD FANTASY

Would you like an ocean view with your enchilada?

The most beautiful Taco Bell in the world sounds like an oxymoron. Fast food restaurants are not usually associated with romantic ambiance, but Pacifica is an exception.

Resembling a beach bungalow, this Taco Bell is located on the sand with a designated surfboard zone in the parking lot. There's no drive-up window; instead, you walk up from the ocean to place your order and the no-shoes no-service rule does not apply.

It's one of a select few Taco Bells with a cantina designation, which means it serves alcohol. Ask the staff to recommend which craft beer, frozen margarita, or rosé best complements your burrito or chimichangas.

Lunch by the indoor-outdoor fireplace is the perfect spot to watch whales breaching, and tables on the deck come with unobstructed views of surfers competing for the perfect wave. When the fog rolls in, no worries; the restaurant sells Taco Bell hats, shirts, and blankets. If you want to feel like the big kahuna, tell your friends the ceiling's murals were created by San Francisco street artist Nora Bruhn.

Good news for out-of-town visitors: there are nearby spots you can shower and rent a surf locker—Traveler Surf Club and simplsurf.com.

With pro surfers like Kelly Slater exchanging boards for clubs, golf is increasingly popular with surfers. The public Sharp Park Golf Course is often called "The poor man's Pebble Beach."

COASTAL CARBS

WHAT: A picturesque Taco Bell

WHERE: 5200 Coast Hwy., Pacifica

COST: Prices start at $1.99.

PRO TIP: For the best views visit in the afternoon after the fog has lifted.

Left: *It's been called the most beautiful fast-food restaurant in the world.*

Right: *Taco Bell is popular with surfers because they work up an appetite riding the waves at Pedro Point.*

Inset: *This fast-food restaurant reserves parking for surfers.*

Afterwards, walking on the beach is peaceful, but if you really want to burn off those nachos there are plenty of more vigorous options, including hiking or biking the panoramic vistas of the rugged coastlines in the Pedro Point Headlands and Mori Point.

29

ETERNAL HOLLYWOOD

Where's the final wrap party in La La Land?

Karie Bible is passionate about old movies, Rudolph Valentino, and a stray black cat who predictably jumps and poses on Cecil B. DeMille's grave as if on cue during her walking tours of Hollywood Forever Cemetery. Bible named him Closeup after Gloria Swanson's line in *Sunset Boulevard*, "I'm ready for my close-up, Mr. DeMille."

Bible loves black; she wears black vintage dresses, carries a black parasol, and on the anniversary of Valentino's untimely death she's one of the ladies in black who mourn the Latin lover. But she refrains from leaving lipstick kisses on his crypt—it leaves a stain.

The cat follows Bible like a puppy as she leads groups to the final resting place of celebrities and lesser-known players in La La Land who still made a big impact, like Herb Jeffries, the first Black cowboy western star.

The largest memorial, a mausoleum in the center of a lake surrounded by bougainvillea, does not belong to a movie star, but rather to the man who started the Los Angeles Philharmonic, William Andrews Clark Jr.

Hattie McDaniel, the first Black woman to win an Oscar, for *Gone with the Wind*, doesn't have a gravesite here because the owners refused her dying wish. When new management came in they built a memorial in her honor.

Bible tells the backstory of the deceased and the Hollywood Forever Cemetery, which is just as intriguing. This

BEYOND THE GRAVE

WHAT: Hollywood Forever Cemetery walking tour

WHERE: 6000 Santa Monica Blvd., Los Angeles

COST: $20

PRO TIP: Wear sunscreen and a hat, and bring water; the tour is 2.5 hours long.

Left: *The cemetery has buildings with mosaics of peacocks which symbolize immortality.*

Right: *Kari Bible with Closeup, who got his name from jumping on Cecil B. Demille's grave during her tours. Photo courtesy of Kari Bible*

Inset: *Mickey Rooney statue looking at mausoleum.*

final resting ground is very much alive, with yoga classes by a reflecting pool and outdoor movies on the grassy lawns. It's also a wildlife sanctuary where swans, ducks, geese, peacocks, and cats roam free. It even has a cat caretaker!

To see living actors, take the Paramount studio tour. You'll spot producers, crew, and talent and speak with archivists as you walk through filming locations and prop warehouses.

BORN IN A BARN

Why did a movie mogul save a shed?

"Hey, kids, let's put on a show!" Classical movie buffs know this line from *Babes in Arms*, when Judy Garland and Mickey Rooney turn a barn into a theater. But most people don't know a barn was the birthplace of the first feature-length movie ever produced in Hollywood.

When Cecil B. DeMille came west scouting locations for *Squaw Man*, he ended up renting a horse barn for his studio. The film was a box-office smash and led to the construction of Paramount Pictures Studio. For sentimental reasons DeMille bought the barn and turned it into a gym for actors on the Paramount lot.

After he died the studio heads wanted to destroy the barn, but it had landmark status so they made a deal with the non-profit Hollywood Heritage...they could have it for a dollar as long as it was moved off the lot. Fortunately for classic movie fans the barn is now the Hollywood Heritage Museum, filled with priceless memorabilia. Each item has a story more intriguing than any moving picture.

In a replica of DeMille's office, you learn his secretary picked up her typewriter and walked out the door when she was told her $15 a week salary would be reduced to $10 due to a new studio policy. DeMille personally made up the difference.

Across the street cannons are pointed at the Hollywood Heritage Museum, but they're friendly fire. The artillery is in front of the American Legion Post 43.

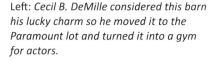

Left: *Cecil B. DeMille considered this barn his lucky charm so he moved it to the Paramount lot and turned it into a gym for actors.*

Right: *Milicent Patrick was the costume designer for* The Creature from the Black Lagoon *but she was ignored until recently. When* The Shape of Water *movie designers borrowed from her techniques she was finally recognized.*

Inset: *Laurel and Hardy were not always making jokes . . . sometimes they were tired like everyone else.*

WHERE HOLLYWOOD BEGAN

WHAT: Hollywood Heritage Museum

WHERE: 2100 N Highland Ave., Los Angeles

COST: $7, free for children under 12

PRO TIP: If you become a member at the $100 level or above, your gift is a 1920s "A Map of Hollywood" poster created by an MGM art director.

Rudolph Valentino quit in a huff when he heard a woman, actor Mary Pickford, was being paid more than The Latin Lover and vintage film cameras were donated by actor James Mason after he discovered a secret screening room in a house he bought from Buster Keaton.

33

RANCHO SHAZAM

Who is Captain Marble?

One man's art is considered junk by some Marin officials. A yellow slide sticking out of a corrugated home, aluminum palm trees, tinmen, and an upside-down bicycle on a tightrope are among the many controversial artworks made of repurposed materials at the Rancho Shazam School of Art and Technical Stuff in Greenbrae.

The owner, Lee Greenberg, a.k.a. Captain Marble, has been sparring with authorities for years but seems to be winning. Recently he says local tourism representatives took photos of his compound.

A former teacher who has always been a tinkerer, he's working on two new outdoor art projects that he says will be the largest in Marin. In the creek fronting his property he's installing a 20-foot-tall, bright-red English metal phone booth equipped with solar lighting so it can be seen from the shore. A 34-foot open Navy vessel is undergoing renovation so it will resemble a fire boat and, in Greenberg's words, it will be the most iconic site on the San Francisco Bay.

If things don't work out in Marin, Greenberg has an escape plan: the Burning Waters Misadventure Park and Marina in Benicia. He bought the land in the hope that artists who create pieces for Burning Man will store them in a giant sculpture garden here and that families will bring their children to the petting zoo.

VISUAL EDUCATION

WHAT: Rancho Shazam

WHERE: 14 Lucky Dr., Greenbrae

COST: Free

PRO TIP: The most scenic way to reach Rancho Shazam is via the ferry. It's a 20-minute walk from the Larkspur terminal.

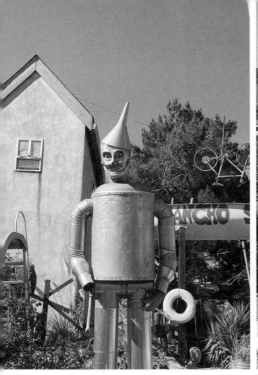

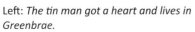

Left: *The tin man got a heart and lives in Greenbrae.*

Right: *Directions are only 5 cents, but who would want to leave?*

Inset: *Rancho Shazam hosts artists who create sculptures from junk.*

While you're in Marin, check out a Cold War museum. The Nike Missile Site, built in the 1950s to target Soviet bombers, is part of the Golden Gate National Recreation Area.

GOING BATTY

What's Batman's worst nightmare?

Bat this idea around: one of the more popular tours in Northern California is a Bat Talk and Walk. That's right, people pay money to visit bat caves.

Caltrans didn't realize when it built a bridge on Highway 80 between Davis and West Sacramento it would become a luxury resort for Mexican free-tailed bats. From mid-June through mid-September these nocturnal creatures hang out in the expansion joint rafters and feast at the all-you-can eat buffet provided by the Yolo wetlands.

Batwoman, a.k.a. Corky Quirk, takes people to see the homes of some 250,000 bats. On the tour she dispels bat myths—no, they're not blind—and leads the group to an area of wetlands not normally open to the public. Here they wait for the bats to gather under the bridge at exit points and stream out in long lines, or ribbons as Quirk calls them. Tours are always successful because bats are creatures of habit. Unfortunately, occasionally one ends up as dinner for a falcon.

Quirk with the Yolo Basin Foundation, finds bats fascinating and laughs that they've taken over her life. "Bats are so misunderstood, and I've always loved the underdog," she says. Farmers encourage bats to hang around by building them houses, because the mammals eat pests that kill crops, saving agriculture billions of dollars each year, according to Quirk. She's also quick to point out that bats are capable of

---

You might see bats in Sacramento's Moon Tree. Astronauts took seeds to the moon and back, and they were planted around the United States, including the State Capitol grounds.

CAPED CRUSADERS

WHAT: Bat Talk and Walk

WHERE: Yolo Bypass Wildlife Area Headquarters, 45211 County Rd. 32B, Davis

COST: Prices vary depending on the package.

PRO TIP: Before you go, apply a generous amount of bug spray.

Top: *The ribbons of bats perform a nightly show. Photo courtesy of Polly Kleinberg*

Inset: *Quirk rescues bats when she's not working and introduces them to her tour groups. Photo courtesy of Polly Kleinberg*

flying up to 100 miles an hour, and "cheetahs get all the credit for being the fastest animal!," she laughs. In her free time Batwoman rescues wildlife, so some lucky groups get to see a live bat up-close and personal.

As for Batman, Quirk says some recent depictions show he's evolved and no longer afraid of the mammal he's named after.

PIG PALACE

Where did pigs live in the lap of luxury?

Acclaimed author Jack London wanted to be remembered not for his books but rather for his farming expertise. London wrote religiously, 1,000 words a day, and became the first American author to earn a million dollars in his lifetime. This adventurer, best known for the books *The Call of the Wild* and *White Fang*, did it all to pay for his Beauty Ranch in the Sonoma Valley.

A "scientific" farmer, London had lots of ideas on improving agriculture, and the park is a monument to many of his mistakes. He saw cattle eating spined cactus in Hawaii and tried this in California but failed. He planted eucalyptus trees thinking they could be used for lumber, but instead they destroyed the soil.

THE BEAUTY RANCH

WHAT: Jack London State Historic Park

WHERE: 2400 London Ranch Rd., Glen Ellen

COST: $10.00 per vehicle

PRO TIP: The park often holds outdoor fundraising events with live performances and wine tastings.

He also built a very expensive pig pen that neighbors ridiculed, but this one wasn't a blunder. London spent $3,000, a fortune in the early 1900s, to build a round stone structure surrounded by pig pens. With a courtyard for each pig family and a roofed sleeping area, a San Francisco newspaper nicknamed it the Palace Hotel for Pigs. This innovative building, which made feeding and caring for the pigs centralized and efficient, cut down on labor costs. When a cholera epidemic hit, London's hogs were saved because he had them walk through disinfectant. The pig palace's metal bars against the walls also prevented moms from accidentally crushing their piglets.

Left: *A reporter said these pigs were living in the animal's version of San Francisco's Palace Hotel.*

Center: *The Park holds outdoor concerts in this stunning setting.*

Right: *The Park's museum has displays on London's talented wife, Charmian.*

The Beauty Ranch, now the Jack London State Historic Park, was home to London and his wife Charmian. They built the Wolf House, but just before moving in the mansion burned down. The remains of their dream house are near his gravesite.

The park includes a museum where you can learn more about the formidable Charmian, an author in her own right and a daredevil who defied societal norms by refusing to ride horses sidesaddle.

Hiking across the property, past vineyards, a lake, and ancient redwood trees, you too might be inspired to pen a few words.

The vineyards are managed by Kenwood Vineyards, and the tasting room is just up the road, a great place to toast the extraordinary lives of Jack and Charmian London.

WALK LIKE AN EGYPTIAN

Where can kids spend the night in a museum?

Silicon Valley, known for its futuristic thinking, is home to a secret society adhering to ancient Egyptian philosophies, such as training your mind to move objects and convincing people to do your bidding.

The national headquarters of the Rosicrucian Order, or Rosy Cross, moved from New York in 1927 because California has always attracted free thinkers, says Executive Director Julie Scott. Cheap land was also an incentive...when Silicon Valley was all orchards, property was reasonable.

Next door the Rosicrucian Egyptian Museum, lined by pillars covered in hieroglyphics, claims to contain the largest number of Egyptian artifacts on exhibit in Western North America. "The biggest misconception is that our artworks are replicas. We have 4,000 authentic relics we collected at a time when we could afford to—in the 1930s," says Scott.

Each year sixth-graders participating in a three-week junior archaeology program are invited to a slumber party, called Night in the Afterlife, where they sleep next to a mummy. In the graduation ceremony they walk through an underground tomb, a replica of a dignitary's crypt in Egypt.

The Rosicrucian grounds include a planetarium; a labyrinth based on the famed one in Chartres, France; a peace garden filled with fragrant flowers and medicinal plants; a reflecting

For inspiration through nature visit the nearby Municipal Rose Garden at the intersection of Dana and Naglee Avenues. It's located in San Jose's oldest neighborhood, with homes dating back to the 1800s.

Left: *The museum holds more Egyptian artifacts than any other place in the US. Photos courtesy of Rosicrucian Egyptian Museum.*

Right: *Children love the sleep among the tombs on the annual "Night in the Afterlife."*

pool; and a research library whose rare books include one by Isaac Newton.

Plans are underway for an alchemy museum, slated to be the largest in the world and the first in the United States, says Scott. Alchemy, the fabled process of transforming lead into gold, is representative of the Rosicrucian philosophy: humans can transform themselves into a higher state of being.

SECRET SILICON VALLEY

WHAT: Rosicrucian Egyptian Museum

WHERE: 1660 Park Ave., San Jose

COST: $10 for adults, $8 for ages 65 and older, students with ID, and children ages 7 to 17, free for ages 6 and younger

PRO TIP: If you're not a child you can still visit the museum at night. Often local organizations take over the museum for fundraising events, allowing attendees to tour the exhibits without the crowds.

DANGEROUS PAINTINGS

Why did a San Francisco artist fear for his life?

Cancel culture is nothing new. In 1953, the magnificent murals Anton Refregier painted on the walls of a San Francisco post office were almost destroyed.

Refregier, who was born in Russia, won a Works Progress Administration (WPA) contest to create art in the Rincon Annex post office. His vision was painting the unvarnished history of Northern California on 27 panels. WWII intervened, and when Refregier returned to work he was under the jurisdiction of the Public Works Administration (PWA) which preferred revisionist history.

Everyone it seemed had an issue...Catholics complained a monk looked too fat next to Native Americans, others disliked the depiction of the cruel conditions the Chinese endured building railroads, but the biggest controversy was his accurate depiction of San Francisco's deadly maritime strike in 1934. The Veterans of Foreign Wars protested the panel, and the *Examiner* newspaper, owned by William Randolph Hearst, fanned the flames until Refregier refused to work at night for fear of getting attacked. The PWA ordered him to cover up the artwork, and in response artists, longshoremen, and warehouse workers protested outside the post office.

Swing by the intersection of Folsom and Spear to see MIRA, the twisty, white high-rise designed by architect Jeanne Gang. She says the spiral shape reinterprets San Francisco's classic bay window.

Top left: *The murals depicted all of society's stratas.*

Top right: *Anton Refregier's ambitious plan was to paint the history of California on the walls of the post office. Photo courtesy of John Williamson*

Bottom left: *Just around the corner, the MIRA building by architect Jeanne Gang is also controversial for some SF residents.*

Bottom right: *Refregier's depiction of the longshoreman's strike caused an uproar in San Francisco.*

THE WORKING MAN'S ARTIST

WHAT: Rincon Center murals

WHERE: 121 Spear St., San Francisco

COST: Free

PRO TIP: Across the street you can see a sculpture honoring the workers who were fatally shot by police during the maritime strike in 1934.

After the murals were finally completed, his troubles were not over. The House Committe on Public Works debated destroying the murals and accused Refregier of being a communist and "too modern."

HURRAY FOR HOLLYWOOD

What million-dollar work of art is underwater?

In 1929 the first Academy Awards took place at the Hollywood Roosevelt hotel, and it was nothing like the Oscars shows today. The ceremony lasted 15 minutes, and all the winners were notified ahead of time.

The location was no doubt selected because Mary Pickford, Douglas Fairbanks, and Louis B. Mayer had spent $2.5 million to build a Spanish style hotel with wrought-iron chandeliers, colorful mosaic fountains, and of course, a pool.

But this is not just any pool. Guests here enjoy a million-dollar swim. The bottom of the Tropicana style pool has a mural of commas that move when guests take a dip. Created by the artist David Hockney it's valued at a million dollars.

Located outside the Hollywood Walk of Fame, Los Angeles's oldest continually operating hotel has plenty of stories. Clark Gable, who was married, occupied the penthouse with a single Carole Lombard; Marilyn Monroe shot her first commercial here—for sunscreen; and Bill "Bojangles" Robinson taught Shirley Temple tap dancing on the tiled staircases. More recently the hotel was seen in the *A Star Is Born* remake with Bradley Cooper and Lady Gaga, *Curb Your Enthusiasm*, and *The Fabulous Baker Boys*.

Go shopping on a silent movie set. The Hollywood & Highland shopping center is built around copies of the four-story Babylon scene from the 1916 film flop *Intolerance*.

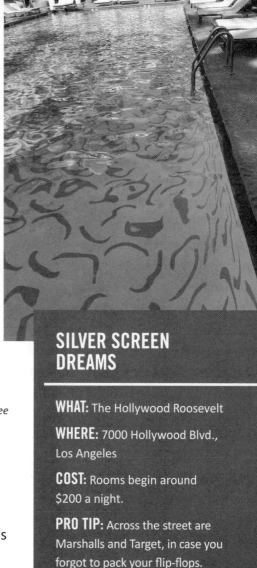

Left: *Bill "Bojangles" Robinson helped Shirley Temple perfect her tap dance on these tiled steps.*

Right: *Dip in the David Hockney pool to see his million dollar artwork move.*

SILVER SCREEN DREAMS

WHAT: The Hollywood Roosevelt

WHERE: 7000 Hollywood Blvd., Los Angeles

COST: Rooms begin around $200 a night.

PRO TIP: Across the street are Marshalls and Target, in case you forgot to pack your flip-flops.

While the Academy Awards have moved on to larger spaces, today the hotel hosts the Golden Raspberry Awards for the worst movies. Late night talk show host Jimmy Kimmel, whose studio is across the street, often has a contest where young people staying in hostels can try to win a night in the Hollywood Roosevelt. Even if they lose they can visit The Spare Room, the hotel's "speakeasy" with a vintage two-lane bowling alley and custom made wooden board games.

REGAL ROLLS

Why does Santa Barbara remind Prince Harry of home?

If your invitation to Meghan and Harry's Montecito soiree was lost in the mail, keep a stiff upper lip. You can always join the Santa Barbara Lawn Bowls Club. After all, if Queen Elizabeth could make the time to stop by during her visit to California in the 1980s, surely you could check out this genteel sport. "I don't think members will ever get over the Queen's visit," chuckles Chris Trenschel, president of Santa Barbara Lawn Bowls Club.

Lilibet had to be impressed by the scenery, palm trees, and classic Spanish architecture set against a backdrop of purple mountains. Under King Henry VIII's reign, lawn bowling was restricted to the aristocracy, with fines for peasants who dared to roll a biased ball toward a target called a jack. Shakespeare wrote about lawn bowling, and that American upstart George Washington played on his father's estate.

The Santa Barbara Lawn Bowls Club, founded in 1937, indulges in the game's rich history. It has a mural of Sir Francis Drake playing a game of bowls in Plymouth, England, even as he saw the invading Spanish armada approaching.

Today the game is open to all classes and ages (it's not a strenuous sport—it has the word bowling in it!), and the dress code is causal...you're not required to wear all white, except on certain tournament days.

If you fancy a spot of tea afterward, visit the Susan Quinlan Doll & Teddy Bear Museum & Library, where toys reveal our history.

Left: *This Sir Francis Drake mural depicts a game he refused to leave despite the Spanish Armada's rapid approach.*

Right: *Santa Barbara has one of the most gorgeous backdrops for lawn bowling.*

Inset: *Lawn bowling has a long tradition with royals.*

BOWLED OVER

WHAT: Santa Barbara Lawn Bowls Club

WHERE: 1216 De La Vina St., Santa Barbara

COST: Free introductory lessons

PRO TIP: You must wear flat shoes to protect the grass.

This city has not one but two lawn bowls clubs; the other is at MacKenzie Park. Perhaps it's because they read *The American Lawn Bowler's Guide*, which advises this activity clears mental cobwebs and is in fact "a veritable fountain of youth."

WILD WEST

What do bikers, bears, and beer have in common?

Just an hour from San Francisco, winding roads overlooking the Carquinez Strait dead-end in Port Costa, a town time forgot. "People make the bend into town and say, 'I can't believe this place exists,' and when they arrive they leave all their stress behind," says Suzanne Statler, cofounder of the planned Port Costa museum.

Surrounded by East Bay Regional Parks, ranches, and the water, this hamlet of 200 can't grow any larger, which suits the residents just fine. They like their unofficial mayor (a musician), picking up mail at the post office, and gathering at a dive bar with a view.

The Warehouse Café was a granary in the 1880s when the city was booming and wheat was transferred via train ferries. Today the dark, cavernous space is filled with taxidermy, including a huge polar bear; mannequins; pool tables; and a bar serving 250 beers in mason jars. On weekends it's a destination for bikers, who come for the outdoor barbeque and live blues. Picnic tables have a view of passing cargo ships, freight trains, hawks, and eagles.

Epicureans walk a few doors down to the Bull Valley Roadhouse, named one of the Bay Area's 100 best restaurants by the *San Francisco Chronicle*.

You can hike or bike to Port Costa along the paved George Miller Regional Trail between Crockett and Martinez.

Left: *Port Costa is along the George Miller regional paved trail.*

Right: *A Doggie Diner head is one of the many eccentric items in the Warehouse.*

HIDDEN HAMLET

WHAT: Port Costa

WHERE: Next to the town of Crockett

COST: Free to walk around

PRO TIP: Stay overnight at the Burlington Hotel, built in 1883. This Victorian inn began when the town was a thriving port.

The shopping here is just as eclectic as the dining. At the Theatre of Dreams, designer Wendy Addison creates stationery on an 1890 letterpress. Shadow puppets, sheet music, satin ribbons, and lace continue the Victorian theme.

Soon the old schoolhouse will become the new museum, and you can't miss it. Just look for the Studebaker fire engine.

HARP (SPEAK) BOONTLING

Why does a small hamlet in Northern California have a secret language?

Pike to Boont for bahl gorms. That's not a typo or a foreign language. It's Boontling, Boonville's homegrown dialect, and means "Travel to Boonville for good food."

Local resident Wes Smith, referred to as the Boont master, is an expert on this secret language. He says it originated in the late 1800s, when the daughter of a San Francisco high society clan found herself "in the family way." She was banished to the Boonville boondocks, and the town's women wanted to talk about the unwed mother without hurting her feelings, so they created a secret language. When the husbands returned home from sheep shearing, they embraced the idea, and soon "everybody got to making up words," says Smith, adding, "You don't just grab in the air and say that's Boontling. It has to be authentic with a story behind it." For instance, shoveltooth means doctor because a local physician with buck teeth had that nickname.

There are only about 1,500 words in the language, often with more than one meaning, and many are derivatives of Native American and Spanish words. Today only about a dozen people still speak Boontling, but locals are doing their best

Practice your Boontling while enjoying Aplenty Bahl Steinber Horn (really great beer) at Anderson Valley Brewing Company. It claims to be the first brewery in the world to offer an 18-hole disc golf course, and it's free!

DON'T HARP ON IT

WHAT: Boontling language

WHERE: Boonville

COST: Free

PRO TIP: Study the language before you visit by reading *Boontling: An American Lingo*. Chico State University professor Charles C. Adams published the book after convincing the locals to trust him with their secrets.

Top left: *If this area looks familiar it was in the movie* Same Time Next Year. *Photo courtesy of VisitMendicinoCounty.com*

Top right: *Take the road less traveled and learn how to speak Boontling. Photo courtesy of VisitMendicinoCounty.com*

Bottom: *Confluence Vineyard where the common language is wine.*

to preserve the language. The Anderson Valley Museum has a Boontling exhibit, radio station KOZT announces a Boontling word of the week, a Boontling opera is in the works, and the Anderson Valley Brewing Company uses Boontling words on its labels.

If someone calls you a bright-lighter, they're most likely talking about someone who lives near the bright lights of the city. "We like to talk about city folk in Boontling, and if they understood some things we say, they'd slap our faces," laughs Smith.

STAGECOACH STOP

How can you travel back in time to the Wild West?

Ah shucks, Santa Barbara ain't all movie stars and royals with their highfalutin ways. Locals don't like to let the cat outta the bag, but they've got a secret hideaway. When they get a bee in their bonnet to grab some grub, they saddle up and head down a twisty road to the old stagecoach stop, Cold Spring Tavern.

Since 1868 these rough hewn buildings have been rustling up chow for weary travelers while the driver changes over to a fresh team of horses. Sakes alive, it was a dangerous, dusty route back then, with hairpin turns and sheer drop-offs. It once took eight hours to get there from downtown Santa Barbara; now it's a lickety-split 20 minutes.

The early owners are a mystery, but in 1941 actress Adelaide Ovington and her husband Earle, the first US airmail pilot, bought the place. Adelaide's daughter Audrey took over in 1972, and since 2005 the third generation of Ovingtons has been running the joint.

COWBOY COUNTRY

WHAT: Cold Spring Tavern

WHERE: 5995 Stagecoach Rd., Santa Barbara

COST: Breakfast and lunch start at $8.25, dinner at $17.50.

PRO TIP: The Old Spanish Days Fiesta, a nearly 100-year tradition, takes place every August with parades, rodeos, and live music.

The ole tavern ain't changed much. They still got hitchin' posts, but these days most folks park their motorcycles, sit on benches made from wagon wheels, and listen to the crick under sycamore trees. Parched cowpokes can wet their whistles with sarsaparilla or hooch at the saloon. It's just like you see in them old Westerns . . . swinging doors, sawdust floors, and gas lanterns.

Left: *Legend has it Roy Rogers pretended to be a bartender here and no one recognized him for 8 hours!*

Right: *Motorcycles have taken the place of horses at this stagecoach stop.*

Inset: *Locals recommend the wild game chili at Cold Spring Tavern.*

Lots of famous folk have stopped by. Merle Haggard had such a rip-roaring time he was 86ed. One time Roy Rogers played bartender for eight hours and no one recognized him! Today's celebrities hide neath their Stetsons and join the shindig every weekend. Modern cowpokes dance to live bluegrass music while tri-tip sandwiches grill on the outside barbeque.

Tenderfoots are welcome here. So, go on now, git.

Continue your cowboy learnin' at the Santa Barbara Carriage and Western Art Museum. It's got the whole kit and caboodle: historic stagecoaches, carriages, and buggies; 50 saddles once owned by celebrities; and purty pictures.

PROPAGANDA POWER

When is art dangerous?

Posters, ashtrays, pincushions, figurines, prayer rugs, playing cards, bottles of lemonade . . . the colorful designs that grab your attention seem harmless, until you look closer. All these objects have messages that could be construed as dangerous.

They're on display at the Museum of International Propaganda in San Rafael, founded by Tom and Lilka Areton. Tom, who grew up behind the Iron Curtain in Czechoslovakia, says growing up he knew he was really an American. At age 20 he was able to leave and met Lilka in New York, where she was volunteering at a social event for foreigners.

Together they formed a student exchange program, and during their travels over 30 years they collected various forms of brainwashing. Sometimes people donate items, such as the American soldier who saved

EXPOSING ADVERTISING

WHAT: Museum of International Propaganda

WHERE: 1000 Fifth Ave., San Rafael

COST: Free, donations appreciated

PRO TIP: If you're connected to a school or senior living facility contact the museum about special tours for these groups.

Mission San Rafael Arcángel is a few blocks away. Founded to assist Mission Dolores in San Francisco, it's named after the patron saint of good health and travelers and is still a functioning Catholic church.

This is the Enemy

Top: *The museum has propaganda posters from all over the world.*

Bottom: *Mixed in with restaurants and boutiques in downtown San Rafael is an unusual museum.*

cartoons from German newspapers while a prisoner of war, and a standing ashtray with a swastika base mysteriously left outside their door.

Most items are from the Soviet Union, Nazi Germany, and communist China, but there are also examples of American propaganda. Novelty items include a Hitler figurine with a pincushion in place of his butt, Ronald and Nancy Reagan slippers, and statues of Mao Tse-tung depicting the Cultural Revolution.

Thursday nights the museum shows rare films, including an anti-CIA movie produced by the KGB. The screenings are free, but there is a small fee to sample Tom's award-winning homemade wine.

HOT MUSEUM

Where can you learn about San Francisco's firefighting history?

Fires have been part of San Francisco from the beginning. There were six fires in 18 months before the 1906 earthquake ruptured gas lines and flames destroyed much of the city. Like a phoenix it rose from the ashes, so San Francisco incorporated this fire bird into the city seal.

With this history, it's not surprising that one of the largest collections of fire memorabilia on the West Coast is in this city. The San Francisco Fire Department Museum is small, but it packs a big punch. It has wagons adorned with intricate artwork, such as the blue pump engine with a painting of the goddess Minerva. If you're lucky they might let you ring the huge bell that warned Chinatown of fires—a bell that cracked during the quake and partially melted. An antique switchboard is so complicated it makes you wonder how they ever got fire crews to the scene.

Visitors learn that San Francisco is the only fire department that uses handcrafted, custom-built wooden ladders. It seems counterintuitive to bring wood to a fire, but here they're safer than aluminum because of the city's low-hanging power lines.

Firefighter helmets, one of the most recognized symbols in the United States, are also on display, along with shields, jackets, and historic photos, including one of Lillie Hitchcock Coit. At age 15 she helped drag an engine to a fire on Telegraph Hill, which got her hooked on hook and ladders. Every time she heard the bell, she ran to help, so firefighters made her an honorary member

THREE ALARMS!

WHAT: San Francisco Fire Department Museum

WHERE: 655 Presidio Ave., San Francisco

COST: Free

PRO TIP: The museum is run by The Guardians of the City and staffed by volunteers so call ahead to make sure it's open.

Top left: *There was a time when horses had to pull fire wagons.*

Top right: *The goddess Minerva is painted on this historic blue pump engine*

Bottom left: *Before cell phones the fire department had a switchboard to transmit calls.*

Inset: *Red emergency fire boxes from the 1860's, located throughout San Francisco, are still in working order.*

of Knickerbocker Engine Company No. 5. In her will she left money for a monument to firefighters, which became Coit Tower. Many people think it resembles a fire hose, but allegedly that was not the architect's intention.

The fire department next door leads tours for educational and community groups by appointment. SFfire.org has all the info on scheduling, but sometimes if you show up on a slow day, they might just show you around.

FREAKS AND GEEKS WELCOME

What is the LA CIA?

Dressed all in black, including his top hat, "the Barnum of Burbank Boulevard" warns visitors waiting near the huge skull not to be afraid as he opens the massive red doors to the California Institute of Abnormalarts. Red lanterns guide your way to the tiki bar, where Barnum, a.k.a. Carl Crew, mixes the cocktail of your choice.

An antiques dealer, actor, writer, producer, and natural showman, Crew loves to show off the treasures he has collected. They include the following:

- An embalmed clown from the early 1900's. (Did I forget to mention that Crew used to be a mortician?).
- A portrait of a French royal who tragically lost his arm. The appendage is on display next to his painting but don't take a picture! He promises to make your wish come true in 24 hours if you leave something of yours behind, but if you took a pic, you're cursed!
- A haunted painting of a woman who visitors swear moves her eyes. Once it was stolen, and the thieves quickly returned it. With a demonic laugh Crew asks, "I wonder what happened to them?"

Drink inside a huge barrel at the Idle Hour. During the 1920s and '30s, there was a trend to create quirky buildings to attract passing motorists. The Idle Hour, one of the few remaining, serves Americana fare and cocktails.

Left: *Clowns, alligator boy and octopus girl greet you at the CIA.*

Center: *If the Barnam of Burbank asks you if you are afraid of heights or boats, say no— trust me you'll be safe!*

Right: *This Jack refuses to stay in the Box.*

CIRCUS SIDESHOW

WHAT: California Institute of Abnormal Arts

WHERE: 11334 Burbank Blvd., Los Angeles

COST: Varies depending on event

PRO TIP: Parking is limited, so it's best to take a ride share.

Crew's love of oddities comes honestly. His uncle Jerry Crew claimed to see Bigfoot, and a plaster cast of Sasquatch's footprints are on display. Every conceivable corner of this cavernous space is stuffed with items from his quirky collection, including a stuffed bear whose eyes light up and who growls when you walk past. Sacha Baron Cohen thought the CIA's outdoor movie theater was the perfect spot to premiere his movie, *Borat Subsequent Moviefilm*.

MUSEUM IN MOTION

How can a museum be one of the biggest and smallest in San Francisco at the same time?

Visitors to the tiny Railway Museum in San Francisco are often surprised it doesn't contain any streetcars. "The museum is our storefront, and the vintage trams outside are museums in motion," says Rick Laubscher, president and CEO of Market Street Railway.

Streetcars were instrumental in growing the city in the early 1900s, went out of favor in the 1950s, and made a triumphant return in the 1980s when cable cars were taken off the streets for badly needed renovations. The city feared this would affect tourism, so it brought back streetcars and scoured the world for vintage trolleys gathering dust to add to their fleet.

The cars, which were repainted in their original colors, have placards in the front window describing their original home and history. The Russian streetcars supposedly carried wounded soldiers in WWII, the open-top boat trolleys were used to transport vacationers to the Irish seaside, and there's a streetcar named Desire from New Orleans.

Get the experience your great-grandparents had sitting on worn wooden seats, feeling the motor rumble below your feet, and watching the fishermen along the waterfront. You might even be on the same streetcar a young woman named Maya Angelou once operated. Legend has it that at age 16 she became the first Black streetcar conductor.

A MOVING EXPERIENCE

WHAT: San Francisco Railway Museum

WHERE: 77 Steuart St., San Francisco

COST: $2.77

PRO TIP: Purchase a Clipper card. It's viable for all modes of transportation in San Francisco, including streetcars, cable cars, ferries, buses, and BART.

Left: *A vintage sign from the era streetcars transformed the city.*

Right: *Jillian Wertzberger is a conductor for the day at the Railway Museum.*

The static museum has a full-size replica of a 1911 streetcar motorman's platform where visitors get to play conductor. You can also see rare photos, travel posters, and 20th-century transit tokens designed by cities across the nation for civic pride. The tokens are displayed in an exhibit called the smallest artifacts in the smallest exhibit in the smallest museum in San Francisco.

To continue this historic transportation theme, visit the free Cable Car Museum at 1201 Mason Street, where you can see the underground machinery that runs this popular form of transportation.

INDULGE IN ILLUSION

Do you believe in magic?

Every weekend in Martinez you're invited to a dinner party. You say you don't know anyone there? Now you do.

Gerry Griffin says visiting the California Magic Club is like coming over to his home for a private, elegant evening; the maximum seating is 40 people. After he and his wife held a successful New Year's Eve party, he decided to open a supper club, don a tuxedo, and welcome people to his place every weekend. He's aiming to re-create the nightclub atmosphere from the '50s, when "everyone dressed up and had a smile on their face."

Walt Disney is his hero, so his magic show is G-rated. "It's an old-fashioned hole in the wall that's fun for the whole family," says Griffin. His family is intricately involved in the venture. Daughter Katy is the chef, and buttonhole relatives (close friends who are like family), make up the rest of the staff.

Between the dinner courses, magicians perform sleight-of-hand tricks at the tables, warming up the audience for the headliners, who Griffin says are "professionals at the top of their game, often coming up from Los Angeles."

Practicing magic, according to Griffin, is mostly a solitary activity. As an only child he spent hours perfecting his craft with the help of TV magic cards. As an adult he opened a magic club and then reinvented the magic show as a dinner theater experience.

TRICKSTERS

WHAT: California Magic Club

WHERE: 514 Main St., Martinez

COST: 89.00 a person for a three-course meal and show

PRO TIP: When in Martinez order a martini. The city claims to have invented the cocktail, and there's a plaque to prove it at Masonic Street and Alhambra Avenue.

Top left: *This old fashioned supper club limits the audience to 40 for a more intimate experience.*

Right: *Magicians come from as far away as Los Angeles to perform in this club.*

Bottom left: *Gerry Griffin loves to surprise his audience.*

Inset: *Magician Larry Wilson dazzling the crowd.*

"I get the biggest kick out of entertaining," says Griffin, who adds, "We always exceed the audience's expectations. They didn't know it would be so much fun."

Martinez claims to be the bocce ball capital of America. There are more than 2000 members in the League who reserve time on 15 courts at martinezboccefederation.com.

ART HOUSE

What is art?

The next time you're inspired to remodel your home, try leaving the broken furniture and scuff marks alone and calling them art. It worked for David Ireland. This leader in conceptual art spent three decades refining his San Francisco Victorian home, and many consider it his masterpiece.

HOME IS WHERE THE ART IS

WHAT: The David Ireland House

WHERE: 500 Capp St., San Francisco

COST: Free

PRO TIP: Ask to see the trapdoor hiding stairs to an underground speakeasy.

Ireland bought the home from an accordion vendor (!) who left behind an enormous safe. When Ireland tried removing the safe it tumbled down the stairs, gauging the walls and floorboards. Instead of covering up the gashes he installed bronze engraved plaques commemorating the day the safe got away.

After peeling away decades of wallpaper and paint to reveal plaster walls, Ireland coated them, along with the ceilings and floors, with high-gloss varnish to reflect the light. When a chair leg broke he didn't try to repair it or throw it away; instead, he declared it a sculpture and hung it on the wall alongside an open red box.

His "chandelier" consists of two blowtorches, and when he repaired the sidewalk fronting his home he videotaped the process and deemed it art. "You can't make art by making art" is one of Ireland's famous quotes. For inspiration he often climbed a steep ladder to the roof, where Ireland was inspired to paint while his children played in the loft.

Left: *When Ireland was not painting on the roof or remodeling his art house he was busy dreaming up his next installation.*

Right: *What to do with a three-legged stool? Christen it a sculpture!*

He was not an overnight success; his art career didn't really begin until midlife. After graduating from the California College of Arts he served in the military, then worked as an insurance agent, a carpenter, an African safari guide and an importer. Eventually he returned home, attended the San Francisco Institute of Art, and became a full time artist.

Following his death in 2009 the Ireland house was opened to the public.

Continue your art appreciation by walking to the nearby murals on the sides of buildings in the Mission district. Balmy Alley and Clarion Alley are home to some of the more vibrant artworks.

RIBBIT

Why are frogs invading the American Riviera?

Santa Barbara, with its Mediterranean weather, dramatic coastlines, sea vistas, and award-winning wine, reminds people of Southern France. So it makes sense that frogs, a nickname for the French, have taken over the city's Riviera neighborhood.

These are not fine-dining frog legs or jumping, croaking, live frogs . . . these are fuzzy, plush, metal, painted, plastic, rubber, wooden, and ceramic frogs sitting on a stone wall.

How this organic outdoor art installation began is a mystery. Some say the owner believed in the feng shui philosophy that frogs attract affluence, so they put one on the wall and neighbors began adding their own frogs.

Others say neighborhood kids used to adorn an alcove with small trinkets, vases, and flowers. After one little boy's ceramic frog was stolen he posted a note begging for his frog to be returned. It was never recovered; instead, dozens of fake frogs were placed there hoping to heal his broken heart. This was in 1989, and the frog collection keeps growing.

FROG SHRINE

WHAT: A wall covered with fake frogs

WHERE: 1600–1714 Paterna Rd., Santa Barbara

COST: Free

PRO TIP: Rumor has it that one frog has a secret compartment containing a note warning that anyone who removes a frog from the shrine will face certain death!

The Santa Barbara Zoo says there are eight local species of frogs in danger of extinction. Residents can participate in FrogWatch, where they identify frogs and toads in their backyard.

Top left: *One little lost his toy frog and people have been leaving him new ones ever since.*

Right: *Who wouldn't want to be a frog in this gorgeous city?*

Bottom left: *Every imaginable frog has been left here.*

The shrine is located in one of the city's swankiest neighborhoods, and locals joke that if Prince Harry and Meghan, who live in nearby Montecito, miss the Frogmore estate in Windsor, they can pay a visit to the Frog Wall. So far there are no confirmed sightings of the royal pair, but Harry has been seen bicycling with his son, and what boy does not want to see a frog wall?

LIQUID GOLD

Why are the French jealous of the Gold Country?

While oenophiles wax euphoric about the golden highlights of certain varietals there is only one winery in California with actual gold. Ironstone Vineyards in Murphys has a 44-pound gold leaf specimen on display, reportedly the world's largest crystalline nugget.

To see the "gold pocket" you walk into a replica of a gold miner's cave. Discovered in nearby Jamestown in the 1990s, it was highly coveted, but Ironstone owner John Kautz successfully outbid numerous international contenders, including the Louvre. Outside the vault his Native American craft collection is on display in the Ironstone Heritage Museum.

This is just one of the many unusual attractions at Ironstone, and the best way to hear the scoop is on an estate tour by Conrad Levasseur. He'll tell you there were 100 wineries in the area during the gold rush as he walks you by the MGM lions and points out a chandelier from San Francisco's Palace Hotel. Kautz was such an avid collector Levasseur says the wine maker once unwittingly bought back items he had donated to a local fundraiser. The grounds tour

DISNEYLAND OF WINE

WHAT: Ironstone Vineyards

WHERE: 1894 Six Mile Rd., Murphys

COST: Estate tours are $10

PRO TIP: If you join the wine club, you get a private bathroom during concerts.

After seeing the wine caves, visit Mercer Caverns, known for its stalagmites, stalactites, flowstones, and the rare white flos ferri.

Left: *Ironstone is also known for its gardens.*

Center: *The dramatic doors are popular with wedding planners.*

Right: *Arbors and gardens line the vineyard grounds.*

Inset: *Conrad Levasseur loves showing visitors the winery's caves.*

is a mini-history lesson the Sierra foothills with reproductions of a mining shack and water wheel.

Ironstone is also an event venue, holding a car show second only to the Concours d'Elegance in Pebble Beach and hosting frequent country and western concerts in the outdoor amphitheater. Many gardeners make a point of visiting each spring when 3,000 daffodils are in bloom.

MANNEQUIN MADNESS

Is there a model in your future?

It all started innocently enough. Judi Townsend was having a hard time finding a mannequin to cover in mosaics and place in her garden. She finally located a former window dresser who had not one, but 50 dummies for sale, and he was going out of business. On impulse Townsend bought his inventory, and although she had spent two decades as a marketing rep for Fortune 100 companies she quit to sell these dummies. When her friends said she was crazy she named the business Mannequin Madness.

Later she learned that when stores get new mannequins, they throw out the old ones, which are not biodegradable. She had a lightbulb idea. Why not help the environment by rescuing these models and selling them?

Customers turn her models into lamps and furniture and use them as coat and hat racks to photograph clothing for sale. They're popular for Burning Man sculptures and Halloween decor. In-store artists turn mannequins into art pieces, including a Da Vinci inspired decoupage dress form recently purchased by actress Rita Moreno.

Her staff began creating headdresses for the mannequins, which led to classes on making floral crowns. For those who don't want to cut down a tree every December, she offers a class on how to turn a dress form into a Christmas tree. The

Show off that new floral headdress at the Dunsmuir Hellman Historic Estate in Oakland, a Neoclassical Revival mansion surrounded by 50 acres of land.

$220.⁵⁰ $180.⁰⁰

A DUMMY COMPANY

WHAT: Mannequin Madness

WHERE: 1031 Cotton St., Oakland

COST: Free to look; prices vary.

PRO TIP: Check out the giveaway pile of mannequins by the front door.

Left: *You can find dummies of all shapes and sizes at Mannequin Madness.*

Right: *Rita Moreno recently bought one of these mannequins inspired by Da Vinci.*

Inset: *Classes on creating headdresses are popular at Mannequin Madness.*

studio can also be rented for "fur-tography" pet pics using her vast array of props.

Mannequin Madness features models of all shapes, sizes, and races, and Townsend, a.k.a. the Mannequin Queen, says she's happy to see more larger sizes being produced.

GALLERY OF GARDENS

Where can you get down to earth?

Yes, the grass is always greener on the other side of this fence, but there's no need for jealousy. Anyone can enjoy the Cornerstone Gardens in Sonoma, which are always green thanks to a natural aquifer.

Inspired by the International Garden Festival in Chaumont-sur-Loire, France, Chris Hougie and Teresa Raffo decided to recreate this concept in the wine country. Landscape architects and designers from around the world compete to create garden installations that are constantly changing.

Currently there are ten displays that connect art, architecture, and nature.

- Rise encourages a walk through a metal tunnel
- Birds flock to the colorful Children's Garden
- Immigrant Tribute has a sheet metal border wallk, a pool of tears and vegetable boxes representing agricultural jobs
- White Cloud has crystals hanging from dark mesh cumulus cloud.

Landscape manager Benjamin Godfrey is proud of the Pollinator Garden designed to attract hummingbirds, bees, and butterflies. "The monarch butterfly population was almost eradicated and now this garden has the highest number of monarchs in Sonoma County," says Godfrey. "It's nice to create habitats." In the future Godfrey is hoping to encourage people from diverse backgrounds to participate in a horticulture competition.

The Cornerstone complex includes shops with decor for your home garden, restaurants, and wineries. Meadowcroft Wines takes advantage of the unique location, leading customers on a sensory stroll through the gardens in preparation for a class on blending their own wine.

Left: *What bird wouldn't want to live here?*

Right: *The gardens are interactive, encouraging you to explore and, in this case, walk through a metal tube.*

STORIED GARDENS

WHAT: Cornerstone Gardens

WHERE: 23570 Arnold Dr., Sonoma

COST: Admission is free; a one-hour tour is $15.

PRO TIP: When you reserve your garden tour, avoid the hottest part of the day, usually 1-3:30 p.m.

Visit Napa Valley's oldest bakery, Butter Cream, established in 1948. The pink and white stripes have been re-painted, but they're still there to welcome customers who crave their traditional recipes.

BLESSED BEACH

When is surfing a religious experience?

Driving down south coast Highway 101 you can't miss the three huge golden lotus domes surrounded by palm trees in Encinitas. They're a jarring sight in this laid-back coastal village, yet it turns out they belong here as much as surf shops, beach bungalows, and taco stands. After all, the man who designed them, Paramahansa Yogananda, is credited with introducing yoga to California.

The domes decorate the Self-Realization Fellowship (SRF) Encinitas Temple. Founded in 1920 by Yogananda, SRF is a spiritual organization that advocates learning from the best of Eastern and Western religions.

A native of India, Yogananda lived for several years at the Encinitas Hermitage, where he wrote *Autobiography of a Yogi*. He often took breaks from this oceanside retreat to walk on the sand and chat with surfers, who named it Swami's Beach in his honor.

SRF grounds include meditation gardens, which are open to the public free of charge. Yogananda pulled out all the stops to encourage reflection, adding plots of roses and begonias, a koi pond, and benches overlooking the Pacific Ocean.

Locals love Surfing Madonna, a mosaic artist Mark Patterson covertly installed under a bridge near a surf spot. When authorities removed it the public protested, and it reappeared on the outside of Leucadia Pizzeria, at the intersection of Highway 101 and Encinitas Boulevard.

Left: *The public is invited to the Hermitage gardens free of charge.*

Right: *Yield for surfers on their way to Swami's Beach.*

SECRET GARDEN

WHAT: Self-Realization Fellowship Encinitas Temple

WHERE: 939 Second St., Encinitas

COST: Free

PRO TIP: Swami's Beach is well-known for large waves, so don't attempt to surf here if you're a beginner.

After your walk, do some retail therapy in the bookstore, where you can buy musical instruments, jewel-toned saris, and Yogananda's book. To this day celebrities embrace Yoganda's teachings. Steve Jobs requested that everyone who attended his memorial receive a copy of *Autobiography of a Yogi*.

PRECIOUS PARK

What was California's most expensive entry fee for a park?

The great outdoors: it's one of the main reasons people love living in California. But until recently, if you visited one park you could wind up in jail.

For more than 50 years, Foothills Nature Preserve was exclusive, just like its zip code. Only Palo Alto residents were allowed to enjoy the hiking trails, lake, and stunning views of the Bay in this pristine park. Outsiders who ventured in were committing a misdemeanor. Since a typical home here costs $3 million according to Zillow, the park's entry fee was astronomical.

Presumably this is not what the land's donor had in mind. Dr. Russell Lee, a revolutionary in health care who founded the Palo Alto Medical Clinic, sold the 1,400-acre parcel to the city in 1958 on the condition it remain undeveloped. According to Steve Staiger, with the Palo Alto Historical Association, in those days the city had grand plans for developing the park, such as adding a merry-go-round. When the surrounding cities refused to help pay for the park's upkeep, Palo Alto closed it to outsiders.

This all changed in 2020, when an NAACP and ACLU lawsuit convinced the city council to allow anyone and everyone to explore the preserve. Larger than Golden Gate Park, with a lake where visitors can kayak, stand-up paddleboard, go canoeing, and

---

For more beautiful scenery, visit the Stanford University campus, home to Frenchman's Tower. Constructed in 1875, no one knows why this French man constructed a two-story brick tower with no doors.

Left: *The city of Palo Alto finally opened their park to the public after a lawsuit claiming discrimination.*

Right: *New visitors are enjoying fishing off the docks.*

OPEN SPACES

WHAT: Foothills Nature Preserve

WHERE: 11799 Page Mill Rd., Los Altos Hills

COST: $6 for parking, free for hikers and bicyclists

PRO TIP: A digital sign on Page Mill Road indicates whether the park is open or temporarily closed due to overcapacity.

fish for bass, it may have been the Bay Area's best-kept secret. Hikers share 15 miles of trails with wild turkeys, deer, bobcats, and coyotes.

To accommodate the increase in visitors, the park now charges $6 for parking and closes when it hits capacity. Still much cheaper than a multi-million-dollar home!

BAKER STREET WEST

Where is Sherlock Holmes' California residence?

Jackson, a California Gold Rush town, could not be more different from London, but at Baker St. West you're transported to Victorian England. Even Scotland Yard would have a hard time finding discrepancies in Baker St. West's reincarnation of Sherlock Holmes' neighborhood.

Linda Hein, an avid mystery reader, and her partner in crime, Beth Barnard, didn't set out to convert a building to all things Sherlockian. They just wanted to form a local chapter of the Holmes Hounds literary society, and it was met with such enthusiasm they created Baker St. West.

On the first floor, The Hein and Co. bookstore has mysteries by Sir Arthur Conan Doyle, but don't try taking one from the twisted stack in the room's center; these books are glued together to form a literary sculpture.

Walking upstairs, the steps are painted with the words, "You see, but you do not observe," a nod to the short story "A Scandal in Bohemia." The second floor is the town square, where you can shop at Dr. Watson's Apothecary, Adler's Emporium, the Deerstalker, Wiggins' Toy Shop, Mrs. Hudson's Tea Shoppe, and South Downs Apiary—a reference to Sherlock's affinity for bees.

Facing the square is 221B Baker Street, the private quarters of Holmes and Dr. Watson. If you accept tea here be aware you may get lost in a hidden door, frightened by a skeleton, or come

If Sherlock is not at Baker St. West you might find him at the National Hotel trying to determine if ghosts do in fact haunt these lodgings.

MYSTERY SOLVED: WHERE DO SHERLOCKIANS GO IN CALIFORNIA?

WHAT: Baker Street West

WHERE: 204 N Main St., Jackson

COST: Free to look; teas are $35.00 a person

PRO TIP: If you're short on time, book a docent-led tour. Baker St. West is a non-profit and requests a $5.00 donation for tours.

Top left: *You can meet Sherlock Holmes, Dr. Watson and Mrs. Hudson at Murder Mystery dinners. Photo courtesy of Farrell Photography/Steve Farrell*

Top right: *Visitors are invited to try and find the many hidden doors. Photo courtesy of Eleanor Caputo*

Bottom: *Investigator Jillian Wertzberger discovers an ear! Just one of the many cases puzzling investigator Sherlock Holmes.*

across macabre evidence on Sherlock's desk, such as a pair of ears from "The Adventure of the Cardboard Box."

Those with a "case most singular" can book a private consultation with Holmes. Night owls might prefer Dinner Mystery Theatre performed by the Baker Street Players, and if all this leaves you wanting more there's a podcast, bakerstreetwest.com

MOD MEDITERRANEAN

Who designed those crazy buildings in the American Riviera?

Tourists in downtown Santa Barbara who walk a few blocks from the surf shops, seafood restaurants, and bicycle rental shacks stumble upon whimsical buildings that stop them in their tracks. In this former Spanish colony, the architecture follows the California mission style. . . with a twist. These white stucco buildings with red tile roofs have melting iron railings covered in tile "blankets," a huge 3-D clock, and colorful illustrated ceramics reminiscent of Gaudi's homes in Barcelona.

They're the brainchild of a Santa Barbara native, architect Jeff Shelton, who says he's oblivious to rules and embraces restrictions. Recreating old Spain "like the rules suggest that we do" is not Shelton's objective. He takes advantage of the fluidity of plaster, which he calls a beautiful melting material, and he designs all the tiles.

He's most famous for Ablitt Tower, a home on a 20-by-20-foot lot. "Everyone said I couldn't do it," says Shelton, who adds that restrictions make you focus quickly. He succeeded, building a tall, skinny tower with about 700 square feet of living space and two kitchens, one indoor and one outdoor. The owners rent the house to visitors, offering a rare chance to see what it's like to live in a Jeff Shelton house.

CALIFORNIA'S GAUDI

WHAT: Jeff Shelton architecture

WHERE: Downtown Santa Barbara

COST: Free to tour on your own. Download here: jeffsheltonarchitect.com/santa-barbara-map

PRO TIP: To support local fundraisers, Shelton leads a few paid tours each year that include the buildings interiors.

Left: *Local artists came together to build the Veracruz building, each of them leaving their signature. Photo courtesy of Jeff Shelton*

Center: *Where Shelton gets his inspiration.*

Right: *At first glance you might think this is a Gaudi building but it's a Jeff Shelton. Photo courtesy of Jeff Shelton*

Shelton is quick to credit local artisans for his success. "I'm like an orchestra conductor," he says. "I design it, but it's an opening. The painters, ceramists, ironworkers, and tile workers are like great musicians playing together. Everyone has talent, and they're often restricted." Shelton says he encourages artists to stand up for what they want while he reminds them of codes and the job's time frame.

A self-guided downtown walking tour highlights eight Shelton projects within six blocks. The location of the buildings contributes to their impact, says Shelton. "You have this focus because you're downtown and playing off the emotions all around you . . . as opposed to being on a ranch somewhere. It's intimate, as though the building is talking to you."

For traditional Spanish-style architecture, check out the self-guided Red Tile Walking Tour at santabarbaraca.com. It includes historic adobes from the 1700s, hidden passageways, theaters, museums, and architecturally significant government buildings.

EGGHEADS

Why are bald heads scattered across university grounds?

It's not what you expect to see on a campus—sculptures poking fun at intellectuals, and incredibly created by one of their own! The late Robert Arneson, a University of California, Davis, art professor, designed five hilarious art installations named Eggheads. These ceramic males are clearly making fun of the ivory tower, and tracking them down is a great introduction to the campus.

Bookhead, appropriately located in front of Shields Library, has a furrowed brow and a nose stuck in an open book. Students reportedly kiss the sculpture for good luck before final exams.

See No Evil/Hear No Evil is positioned, perhaps ironically, across from the School of Law.

Stargazer, smiling and looking toward the sky, is south of Young Hall, where students study psychology, sometimes referred to as navel-gazing.

The smiling Eye on Mrak is an upside-down head laughing on one side, with an eye staring at the administration building, Mrak Hall. It's named after the second chancellor, Emil Mrak, an avid cyclist responsible for making the campus bike-friendly. This is the most popular Egghead to show up in photographs.

Wright Hall, devoted to the performing arts, is home to Yin & Yang, which Arneson said is about passiveness and aggressiveness. "The one lying on its side is in kind of a reflective

Because the Arneson estate retained rights to the Eggheads, you may see replicas elsewhere, such as Yin & Yang on the Embarcadero in San Francisco.

Left: *Sydney Robinson, a new student at UC Davis, shows her love for the Aggies.*

Right: *Arneson saw all sides to life. Photo courtesy of Arneson trust*

BRAINY BUSTS

WHAT: Egghead sculptures

WHERE: Scattered across University of California, Davis

COST: Free

PRO TIP: Arneson's UC Davis contemporary was the artist Wayne Thiebaud. Most famous for his paintings of cakes and pies, he was a popular professor at UC Davis for 40 years.

state, but it is looking backward, because the other head is lecturing or interrupting him. It's more intense," said Arneson.

Beyond the Eggheads, Arneson was a pioneer in the Funk art movement that poked fun at everyday objects such as toothbrushes and toasters. He is known for elevating ceramics from the craft world into an independent art form.

RESEARCHING BIGFOOT

Who's looking out for Sasquatch?

Bigfoot is not joke to Michael Rugg. After he was laid off from his Silicon Valley job in 2004, this Stanford grad decided to "do his own thing" and devote himself to studying Sasquatch. "Bigfoot people have been frustrated because they're not able to prove Sasquatch exists, so I've dedicated all my time to it," Rugg says.

STUDYING SASQUATCH

WHAT: Bigfoot Discovery Museum

WHERE: 5497 Hwy. 9, Felton

COST: Free, donations appreciated

PRO TIP: Reserve a private tour; it's only $5. And don't forget to take a photo in front of the nine-foot-tall Bigfoot statue.

When he opened the Bigfoot Discovery Museum in Felton "locals said you don't have to look far for Bigfoot, they're right here in our backyard!" A map in the museum has colored pins marking 150 spots people say they saw these "big hairy people with a language," according to Rugg, who adds "they've been avoiding us since the bow and arrow trounced hand-to-hand combat."

Rugg's obsession dates back to a childhood sighting of Bigfoot. While camping with his parents he wandered off and saw "a creature who looked like the incredible hulk, with a shirt hanging off him in tatters."

The museum has a continuous loop of the famed Patterson film purportedly showing Big Foot, plaster cast foot imprints, and

After getting insider tips at the museum, try to sight Bigfoot yourself in the Big Basin Redwoods State Park. Even if you're not successful, it's a beautiful place to hike.

Left: *The huge Bigfoot statue is a favorite with Instagrammers.*

Inset: *Michael Rugg went from a tech job to studying Bigfoot. Photos courtesy of the Bigfoot Discovery Museum*

several Bigfoot statues. In 2020 someone stole the four-foot sculpture nicknamed Danny—because it looked like Danny DeVito—from the entrance. The police issued a bulletin asking people to be on the look for Bigfoot—no, seriously, Bigfoot. Days later Danny was found stranded by the side of the road.

Serious as Rugg is about Bigfoot, he has a sense of humor. The museum displays Bigfoot toys, lunch boxes, and tabloid cover stories about the creature. There is also a paranormal display of Bigfoot—does Elon Musk know about this?

NATURAL ART

Why does San Francisco encourage you to destroy some art?

Some sculptures in San Francisco are slowly falling apart, and that's OK with the artist. Nature is Andy Goldsworthy's muse: he transforms twigs, leaves, and fallen trees into artworks that blend into the woods and will eventually return to the earth. Unlike most artists, he wants people to not only touch his artwork but jump on it.

Children love walking on the serpentine *Wood Line* that Goldsworthy created from fallen eucalyptus trees near Lovers' Lane, the Presidio of San Francisco's oldest footpath and often used by couples for engagement photos. Installing this was a delicate operation because the location is a federally designated historic forest. The Presidio of San Francisco is a former army base, and its trees were planted by the US military beginning in the late 1800s.

Balancing on the logs, you can see another of Goldsworthy's sculptures, *Spire*, which was formed from cypress trees cut down for reforesting. A triangle rising 90 feet in the air, it's often compared to a church steeple.

His only indoor exhibit is a eucalyptus tree trunk covered in human hair. *Tree Fall* is located in the tiny Powder Magazine building, named for its original use, storing gunpowder during the Civil War. *Tree Fall* is intended to make people think about the relationship between what's natural and what's man-made.

FOREST FINERY

WHAT: Andy Goldsworthy art

WHERE: Presidio of San Francisco, 103 Montgomery St., San Francisco

COST: Free

PRO TIP: Presidio.gov has a map of Goldsworthy artwork throughout the park.

Left: *While you walk around the Presidio to see Goldworthy's art, stop to admire the views.*

Right: *Unlike most artworks, these sculptures are meant to be touched— even walked on.*

Inset: *There is a Buffalo Soldiers' cemetery in the Presidio.*

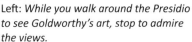

Beyond the Presidio you can also see Goldsworthy's work at the de Young Museum in San Francisco. At the entrance, *Drawn Stone* has a large crack running across the courtyard reflecting the city's earthquake history.

While you're at the Presidio, visit the Buffalo Soldiers section in the National Cemetery's Spanish-American War area.

SACRAMENTO'S SECOND CITY (page 130)
Photo courtesy of Sacramento History Museum

FELICITATIONS (page 4)

FREAKS AND GEEKS WELCOME (page 58)

THORNBURG VILLAGE (page 170)

HARP (SPEAK) BOONTLING (page 50)

LIQUID GOLD (page 68)

일심단결

PROPAGANDA POWER (page 54)

METAMORPHOSIS (page 132)

TROLLING (page 182)

SURF ART (page 166)
Photo courtesy of Andy Robinson

PRESIDENTIAL PENTHOUSE (page 164)
Photo courtesy of the Fairmont Hotel

MOD MEDITERRANEAN (page 80)
Photo by Jeff Shelton

ROCK STAR (page 136)

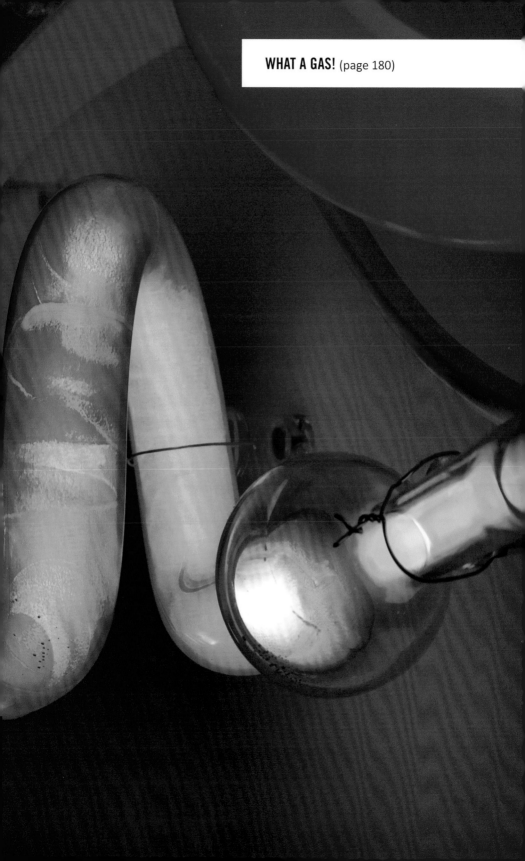

WHAT A GAS! (page 180)

BAKER STREET WEST (page 78)

REGAL ROLLS (page 46)

SCENTSIBILITY

What does whale excrement smell like?

The country's first perfume museum, the Aftel Archive of Curious Scents, happens to be located behind another olfactory treasure, Alice Waters' Chez Panisse restaurant in Berkeley. It's serendipitous because the museum's founder, Mandy Aftel, has consulted with Michelin chefs, the cannabis industry, and vintners on scents...which she says age like fine wine.

Aftel understands people's primal response to smells, and her museum is an interactive experience designed to wake up that sense. Her museum unpacks the complexity of scent by bringing it down to earth. Visitors touch raw materials such as bark, roots, frankincense, and myrrh to see the connection between plants and scents. You can smell more than 300 natural essences from grasses, fruits, flowers, and trees.

"It's an archive museum of scents, not finished products like perfume, although I am a perfumer," says Aftel. "It's an astounding aromatic rainbow of materials."

Much like smelling coffee beans at a winery helps you reset your olfactory system, you're given a piece of felt to inhale in between the "smell me" bottles.

At the perfume organ you're encouraged to experiment with the various categories of scents, such as floral and woodsy, and discover a fragrance's top, middle and base notes. When you leave you take home three personalized scent strips.

GET NOSEY

WHAT: Aftel Archive of Curious Scents

WHERE: 1518 1/2 Walnut St., Berkeley

COST: One-hour time slots are $20 ($12 for kids under 18).

PRO TIP: If you're interested in buying one of her natural perfumes, Aftel encourages customers to buy a sample first to see how the fragrance reacts with your skin.

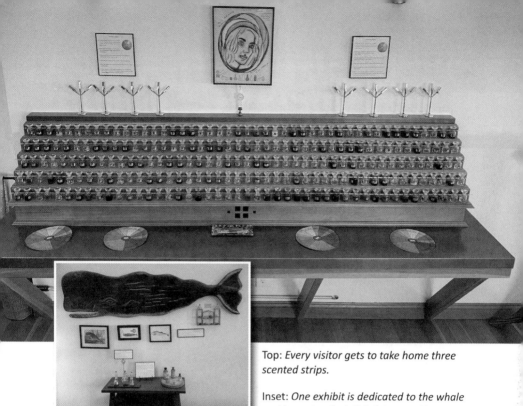

Top: *Every visitor gets to take home three scented strips.*

Inset: *One exhibit is dedicated to the whale and its curiously delightful scent. Photos courtesy of Foster Curry*

A collector of rare scents, Aftel has many bottles over a hundred years old that were never opened until she purchased them at pharmacies. The most unusual has to be ambergris or whale excrement she gets from New Zealand...and it happens to be one of her best-selling fragrances.

Keep your sensory exploration going by visiting the Berkeley Rose Garden. There are 1,500 rosebushes to smell while enjoying views of the San Francisco Bay and the Golden Gate Bridge.

OUR LADY OF TOUCHDOWNS

Why is there a huge statue of the Madonna in the middle of Silicon Valley?

When 49er football players need a Hail Mary pass, inspiration is just down the road: a 32-foot-tall silver statue of Christ's mother in front of our Lady of Peace Church in Santa Clara. The stainless steel shrine, as tall as a three-story building, seems out of place in Silicon Valley, better known for tech zealots than the religious faithful.

In the early 1980s Monsignor John J. Sweeny was anxious to attract more parishioners and thought erecting a giant sculpture of the Virgin Mary, visible from the new Highway 101, was the answer.

His superiors forbade him from asking for money, so he asked for prayers . . . and it worked. The community contributed enough for artist Charles Parks to create The Immaculate Heart of Mary statue. One of only three Marian shrines on the West Coast, it made Our Lady of Peace Church a religious destination.

Catholics from around the world make pilgrimages to see "Our Lady of Silicon Valley," laying flowers at her feet, walking the outdoor Stations of the Cross, and picnicking under umbrellas on the lush lawn surrounded by rose gardens.

Across the street, Mission College (a state community college—not religious, despite the name) has a population of rare owls that burrow underground. Look for the signs indicating the homes of these unusual birds.

The devoted lay flowers at this Marian shrine.

RELIGIOUS INTERCEPTION

WHAT: Our Lady of Peace Shrine

WHERE: 2800 Mission College Blvd., Santa Clara

COST: Free

PRO TIP: If you buy a candle in the bookstore, you can have it blessed by a priest.

On the anniversary of the Marian apparitions in Fátima, Portugal, when three children said they saw the Mother of God, the church holds special masses replicating Portugal's ceremonies, complete with candlelit rosary processions and the blessing of the sick. Many parishioners claim miracles have taken place during these ceremonies.

UTOPIA IN TIBURON

Why is there a stone tower in Tiburon?

Around 1889 Dr. Benjamin Lyford, a Civil War physician and inventor of an embalming fluid, urged people to take up residence near "the fountain of youth and health." Lyford's Hygeia, or Goddess of Health, was the first subdivision in California, and "only those of unimpeachable character" would be allowed to live here, so as to keep out "vices and vampires."

The housing development had strict rules.... no alcohol, tobacco, dancing, or gambling. When this dismayed prospective buyers, Lyford said sinners could indulge their vices in the privacy of their homes.

His ambitious plans were possible due to a fortuitous marriage to Hilarita Reed, one of his patients at his San Francisco practice. Reed inherited large tracts of land in Tiburon that were "free from fog and malaria," according to the 1989 brochure for Lyford's Hygeia. As proof of the area's excellent climate, the brochure said, "A large number of women's ailments have been cured by taking up residence there."

Originally the Norman-style tower was a small office and the gateway to the resort, but today all that remains is the open stone structure offering unobstructed views of the Bay and the San Francisco skyline.

FOUNTAIN OF YOUTH

WHAT: Lyford's Stone Tower

WHERE: 2034 Paradise Dr., Tiburon

COST: Free

PRO TIP: To preserve your health, take the leisurely, stress-free journey to Tiburon aboard a ferry.

Left: *The tower is all that remains of Lyford's Hygeia.*

Right: *Taking the ferry is the easiest and most beautiful way to reach Tiburon.*

It's a national historic landmark, and so is Lyford's home, which is managed by the Richardson Bay Audubon Center. In 1957, it was still in the original location, the Lyford's' dairy on Strawberry Point, and in danger of being demolished, but preservationists moved it across the Bay on a barge to Tiburon.

It's too late to join Lyford's Hygeia, but you can pray for good health at Old St. Hilary's Church, 201 Esperanza St. in Tiburon. A landmark, it was built as a place of worship for railroad workers in 1888.

MARINA MOODS

What are those huge heads doing in the front yard?

Most of the bikers, walkers, and drivers along the Marina Green are gazing at the sailboats gliding across the bay, but a lucky few turn around and notice a colorful sculpture garden in front of a stucco home. It's a jarring sight: huge heads peeking through the bushes, a rooster, and a woman on a bench with a cellphone seemingly monitoring the neighborhood.

"Wherever you go in the world, you see things if you walk you would never see while driving," says the homeowner Art Scampa. The free, fun art is a gift to passersby from Scampa, a retired lawyer who took up sculpting as a hobby. His community college instructors, impressed by his innate talent, were surprised he was a neophyte. "My grandfather was an Italian stone sculptor. I never knew him, but maybe I got some of his talent," laughs Scampa.

There was no grand scheme to his display; he just kept firing the kiln. Travel inspires his art, particularly to Italy. One of his favorites is the woman on the bench, modeled after his late mother, so realistic many think it's a live person.

NEVER HOME ALONE

WHAT: Sculpture garden

WHERE: 325 Marina Blvd., San Francisco

COST: Free

PRO TIP: If you're looking for love visit the Marina Safeway, dubbed Dateway.

After admiring Scampa's sculptures, experience culinary art at Fort Mason, home to Greens, the oldest vegetarian restaurant in San Francisco.

Left: *It's not your imagination-people are watching you in San Francisco's marina*

Right: *Passersby think this is a real person—it's a statue of Scampa's mother.*

Inset: *Scampa's art instructors were impressed with his innate talent.*

"If my wife is doing yardwork, kids go totally bananas," says Scampa, adding that the neighbors love the free museum. "It's great when you make people happy—sometimes I go out and look at it and say to myself, how did I do that?"

CARMELOT

Where do you need a permit to wear high heels?

In this modern-day Camelot, thatched cottages on cobblestone streets don't have numbers but rather names like Periwinkle, and residents must collect their missives at the post office to meet their neighbors. Every so often politicians put mail delivery on the ballot, only to have residents vote a resounding no, says Sandra Book, director of tourism for Carmel-by-the-Sea or, as I call it, Carmelot.

If you live here, there's no need to bring filthy lucre to the grocery store; customers just sign for their caviar and champagne. Streetlights are strictly forbidden. Traffic lights and parking meters don't exist in Carmelot. As the late Richard Burton sang in the movie *Camelot*, "I know it gives a person pause, but those are the legal laws."

BLISSFUL BEACH

WHAT: Carmel-by-the-Sea

WHERE: About two hours south of San Francisco

COST: Free to walk the white sand beach

PRO TIP: The La Playa hotel bar has 10-cent drinks whenever the bartender is feeling generous. When you hear the bell, rush to the bar—the deal ends five minutes later.

You need a special dispensation to wear high heels here, because the city is afraid of lawsuits from women who fall on the cobblestones. The free permit, available at city hall, is a popular keepsake requested by many visiting celebrities. I know it sounds a bit bizarre but that's how conditions are in Carmelot.

Movie stars love Carmelot . . . and why not? In Carmelot the climate must be perfect all the year and man's best friend is treated like royalty. The entire village pampers dogs with treats and bowls of water outside stores. The late Doris Day is credited with starting the first pet-friendly hotel here, the Cypress Inn. Don't miss yappy hour, which coincides with a human happy hour.

Left: *Just like Camelot the weather is almost always perfect in Carmelot. Photo courtesy of John Williamson*

Right: *You could mistake Carmel by the Sea for an English village. Photo courtesy of CarmelCalifornia.com*

Inset: *Many credit Doris Day with starting the dog-friendly hotel concept. Photo courtesy of CarmelCalifornia.com*

Another movie star, Clint Eastwood, is often spotted playing piano at the hotel and restaurant he owns, Mission Ranch. Formerly the mayor, one of his campaign promises was to reverse the ban on eating ice cream cones on the street—locals were dismayed by scoops falling on pristine sidewalks.

In short, there's simply not a more congenial spot for happily-ever-aftering than here in Carmelot.

Relive the bohemian days of Carmelot at the Robinson Jeffers Tor House. A California poet, Jeffers built his stone house and tower in the early 1900s. Jack London and other artists pitched tents on the beach and cooked abalone . . . no doubt breaking many of Carmelot's current laws!

ROMAN HOLIDAY

Who has the golden touch?

Before Burning Man existed, art students in the San Francisco Bay Area had their own creative gathering each May Day at Waddell Creek in Santa Cruz. When 19-year-old Annie Morhauser saw a student using a portable glass-blowing furnace on the beach under a full moon, she discovered her life's work. "It lit a passion in me," says the founder of Annieglass.

While "messing with" the surface of glass at the California College of the Arts, Morhauser developed her own version of the ancient glass-forming process called slumping. She painted 24-karat gold on the rims of thick glass plates and bowls, made them dishwasher safe, and called the technique Roman Antique. Annieglass, which has graced the tables of presidents and movie stars, is now on permanent display in the Smithsonian American Art Museum.

This self-described hippie was concerned about leftover glass being thrown away, so she developed an Elements series that uses only recycled glass. Her factory in Watsonville offers free tours, where you can watch artisans at work and find bargains in the seconds store, where pieces with barely perceptible mistakes sell at a fraction of the retail price.

If all this is inspiring your inner artist, Annieglass has a Craftbar where you can draw and drink wine. She invites local artisans to teach their craft, such as leather making or watercolors. One of the most popular classes is how to make a succulent garden with an Annieglass planter.

MODERN ANTIQUES

WHAT: Annieglass Studio

WHERE: 310 Harvest Dr., Watsonville

COST: Tours are free

PRO TIP: Morhauser's son Taylor Reinhold is an accomplished artist in his own right. You can see his murals all over Santa Cruz.

Top left: *Annie Glass became famous for creating dishwasher safe plates lined with gold.*

Top right: *Annieglass offers free tours of the factory in Watsonville.*

Bottom left: *Annie Morehauser in front of a kiln at her Watsonville factory.*

Bottom right: *Annie Morehauser with her daughter Ava at the Craft Bar.*

Morhauser is proud to say Annieglass is a woman-run business, with her daughter and daughter-in-law as the other two women in charge. She designs two new sustainable, handcrafted collections a year, but her bestseller continues to be the original Roman Antique line.

Continue your artistic adventure by touring The Apple Crate murals. Several local artists have painted these vibrant vintage advertising labels on the sides of buildings throughout Watsonville.

CHICKEN BOY

Where is the LA version of the Statue of Liberty?

This is a love story about a lonely woman in La La Land and a Chicken Boy statue. When Amy Inouye moved from the San Francisco Bay Area to Los Angeles, she felt adrift, but a huge fiberglass sculpture on top of a Chinese restaurant on Broadway brought her comfort.

Chicken Boy reminded her of the Doggie Diner heads advertising hot dog restaurants in the Bay Area. As a kid she fixated on those dogs spinning around, so when she moved south this SoCal advertising icon spoke to her.

"It's hard to describe," she says, "but Chicken Boy made me feel comfortable . . . he was my welcoming committee to Southern California." When the restaurant closed, she asked what would happen to "LA's Statue of Liberty." She kept bugging them, and eventually they said, "Why don't you take him?"

This graphic designer took ownership of Chicken Boy, but the course of true love never did run smooth. Inouye didn't

IT'S OKAY TO BE CHICKEN HERE

WHAT: Chicken Boy statue and store

WHERE: Future Studio Gallery, 5558 N Figueroa St., Los Angeles

COST: Free to look; merchandise prices vary

PRO TIP: If you'd like a mini Chicken Boy in your home, check out the website, chickenboyshop.com

You might see a live chicken at the nearby Audubon Center at Debs Park, dedicated to restoring habitats for birds and other wildlife.

Left: *Chicken Boy has been called the Statue of Liberty for Los Angeles.*

Right: *Amy Inouye installing her Chicken Boy. Photo courtesy of Gary McCarthy*

realize how difficult it would be to find him a home. She was planning to donate him to a sculpture garden, but no takers. Finally the city planning commission gave her permission to place him on the roof of her graphic design business, and in return Chicken Boy allowed her to sell merchandise in his likeness.

Her business is along historic Route 66 in the hip Highland Park area, so she gets visitors from around the world who want to meet her boyfriend. As you'd expect of a star, Chicken Boy has a fan club on Facebook.

SASSY SWINE

Why do pigs love this beach?

Oink oink, I smell bacon. This is among the silly phrases uttered when someone sees a police officer. One Santa Barbara homeowner who was married to a cop decided to have fun with this and create a pig monument to her late husband. The front yard of the "pig house" is filled with swine; a pink pig with a dollar sign, a steel pig, and a pig maître d' are just a few of the art pieces.

The "Pig House Lady" says some of the "hotsy-totsy" residents don't appreciate her display, but she doesn't care. "Pigs are amazing, and people like to make pigs. Pigs are happy," she says. She's proud of her collection of over 6,000, and says: I don't know what happened, but I keep adding to it. In case you're wondering, she doesn't have a pet pig but does occasionally eat roast pig, even though she was raised kosher.

People riding segways, bicyclists, walkers, and children all stop and stare at her yard, but they don't get to see the best of her collection. Inside there's a six-foot-tall pig on roller skates she calls Bess in honor of her grandmother, and a pig pillbox created by a famous purse designer.

A business manager in the movie business, she finds her pigs on her travels all over the world, and laughingly admits to being a catalog addict. There are no duplicates. They are all individual, and she envisions the collection will someday become a museum. In the meantime, you can admire them on your way to Butterfly Beach.

THIS LITTLE PIGGY WENT TO THE BEACH

WHAT: The Pig House

WHERE: 80 Butterfly Ln., Santa Barbara

COST: Free

PRO TIP: This is a private residence, so be respectful of the owners.

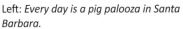

Left: *Every day is a pig palooza in Santa Barbara.*

Right: *No, the chef said pork is not on the menu.*

Inset: *The pig collection started as a joke; the owner's husband was a police officer.*

Continue walking toward the Biltmore to see the Coral Casino Beach and Cabana Club featured in the mystery novels of Ross Macdonald. The Coen brothers have optioned his book Black Money.

HEAVEN CAN WAIT

Where can you grow young?

After "The Big One," a.k.a. the 1906 earthquake, the movers and shakers of San Francisco relocated to the burbs, which they thought were safer. One sumptuous estate from that era is still intact: Filoli in Woodside, ironically built along the San Andreas earthquake faultline.

The unusual name was invented by the owner, William Bourn II, who combined letters from his motto, "Fight for a just cause, love your fellow man, live a good life." Bourn, who made his money the old-fashioned way—inheriting the Empire gold mines—told friends Filoli was his refuge where he intended to "grow young."

In a few hundred years, he prophesied, the estate would prove interesting, and each year 230,000 visitors agree. You may have seen Filoli on the TV show *Dynasty* or the movies *Heaven Can Wait*, *The Joy Luck Club*, and *The Wedding Planner*.

Renowned San Francisco architect Willis Polk, best known for the Hallidie building, the first structure with a glass curtain wall many say was the precursor to the modern skyscraper,designed this 36,000-square-foot red-brick Georgian Revival mansion, which naturally has a ballroom and servants' quarters. The manicured gardens, though, are the real draw. They include a rose garden, sunken garden, and walled garden, and many have reflecting pools.

GROUNDED

WHAT: Filoli Historic House and Garden

WHERE: 86 Cañada Rd., Woodside

COST: $25

PRO TIP: Fans of *The Crown* will be delighted to hear that private tea services can be arranged.

Left: *Stepping into the Filoli estate is like going back in time.*

Right: *Bourn intended to grow young at this home.*

Inset: *People come from all over the world to see the flowers in bloom at Filoli.*

Filoli was later purchased by the Roths, who eventually opened the estate to the public. Their twin daughters, Lurline and Berenice, often surprised guests by giving impromptu tours.

Woodside is also home to the Djerassi Ranch, an artist-in-residence program. Members of the public can admire the sculptures and installations by signing up for free art hikes.

TACKY TITANS

How did so many giants end up in Hayward?

You don't expect to see towering cowboys, lumberjacks, and spinning dog heads wearing chef hats and bow ties in an industrial area, but Bell Plastics in Hayward has all this and more. The owner, Bruce Kennedy, collects these massive fiberglass figures, which were originally used to advertise various businesses.

The collection began when Kennedy noticed that a carwash in Hayward with a 20-foot statue of a lumberjack was going out of business. He asked if "Big Mike," as he called it, was for sale.

He was, and soon Kennedy tracked down friends for Big Mike from all over the country, including a giant nicknamed Hollywood in a Hawaiian shirt, a firefighter, an Amazon-sized woman originally used to advertise Uniroyal tires, a Gas Guy who promoted gas stations, octopi, dinosaurs, Santa Claus, and a Burger Boy.

Kennedy restores the originals and makes molds to sell replicas. "We sold a customized statue, and the day the customer put it up his business doubled and has doubled ever since. It's in the middle of nowhere, and it paid for itself in 21 days. I would sell more if cities didn't say no . . . some people think they're tacky," sighs Kennedy.

After you see the giants, often called muffler men, visit the final resting place of Karl Becker, the diminutive "Mayor of Munchkinland" in *The Wizard of Oz*. He is buried at the Lone Tree Cemetery in Hayward.

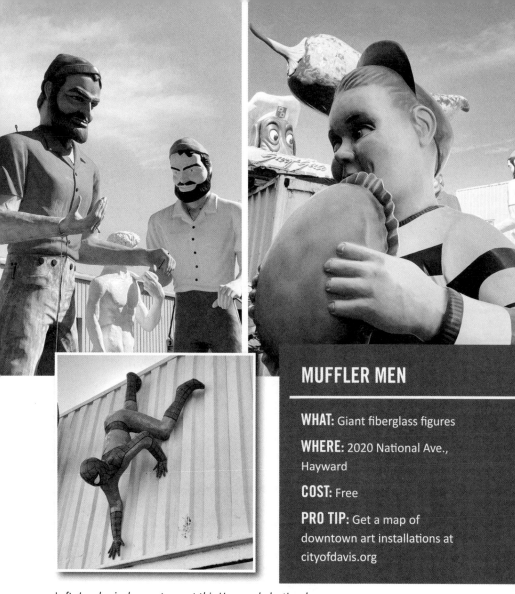

MUFFLER MEN

WHAT: Giant fiberglass figures

WHERE: 2020 National Ave., Hayward

COST: Free

PRO TIP: Get a map of downtown art installations at cityofdavis.org

Left: *Lumberjacks greet you at this Hayward plastics shop.*

Right: *Many of the statues were used to entice motorists to visit restaurants.*

Inset: *There are even superheroes in case someone needs rescuing in Hayward.*

The advertising icons need a lot of care, but Kennedy doesn't mind. "We're hogging them," he laughs. People come from all over the world to see the collection, and at his last open house 3,000 people came to admire the tacky titans.

DOG AND CAT SHOW

Can anyone create a masterpiece?

New students at the University of California, Davis, often miss the pets they left at home, but there's good news. Roy the Dog and Calico Cat are there for them.

These huge sculptures, built by volunteers, pose in front of the John Natsoulas Center for the Arts. Like Tom Sawyer, Natsoulas asks everyone to join in the fun of creating art. Instead of asking passersby, however, students put out the word on social media. Natsoulas says the volunteers didn't need to know anything about constructing a sculpture; his team of professional artists was there to guide them.

Roy the Dog was the first large-scale installation, an homage to the late UC art professor Roy De Forest, a mentor to Natsoulas, who often included dogs in his art. Roy was built of tin boxes, vinyl records, and other recycled materials, and Natsoulas says it lights up at night like a beacon. "We were going to move it," says Natsoulas, "but the community balked."

A CREATIVE COMMUNITY

WHAT: Roy the Dog and Calico Cat

WHERE: 521 First St., Davis

COST: Free

PRO TIP: Get a map of the art around downtown Davis at cityofdavis.org.

Davis has a long history of community involvement. Across the street volunteers built the Boy Scouts log cabin in 1927. The logs are actually electrical poles donated by PG&E.

Left: *Roy the Dog and the Calico Cat stand guard outside the John Natsoulas Gallery in downtown Davis.*

Right: *Natsoulas used antique tiles to build the Calico Cat.*

When his friend's kitty died, Natsoulas acquired orange tile from the 1940s to build a friend for Roy, a blocky calico cat. "If you can figure out how to do things that don't cost a lot, you can do a lot of things," says Natsoulas. His community art projects, located all over town, are part of the Davis Transmedia Art Walk, the world's first interactive art walk. An embedded chip in each mural and sculpture enables visitors to see videos about the work's construction.

The John Natsoulas Center for the Arts has frequent educational and cultural events, such as live music, poetry readings, and theater, often on the rooftop deck.

WATER WORSHIP

What is a Greco-Roman temple doing in the middle of nowhere?

"Oh Girls! Get Set for Hetch Hetchy Hair," read a 1934 San Francisco Chronicle headline. It was something to celebrate after the Great Depression: the Bay Area finally had reliable, inexpensive water, ending a monopoly by the Spring Valley Water Company.

After 24 years and more than $100 million, melted snow from the Hetch Hetchy mountains in Yosemite found its way to the Bay Area. Simple gravity moved the aqueduct's water more than 160 miles.

To commemorate this engineering marvel, thousands gathered in Redwood City and cheered as water roared to the new Pulgas Water Temple. This Beaux Arts monument was designed by architect William Merchant, who also worked with Bernard Maybeck on the Palace of Fine Arts. Merchant's design reflected the architecture of the ancient Greeks and Romans, whose aqueduct methods had inspired San Franciscans.

Fluted Corinthian columns are reflected in a pool surrounded by cypress trees. The ceiling of the temple is encircled with a biblical inscription: "I give waters in the wilderness and rivers in the desert, to give drink to my people."

If you're wondering about the name Pulgas, the land is a former Spanish Land Grant called Rancho de las Pulgas.

Today tap water in the Bay Area is considered among the cleanest in the nation, so be sure to fill up your water bottles at various stations.

WATER MARKS

WHAT: Pulgas Water Temple

WHERE: 56 Cañada Rd., Redwood City

COST: Free

PRO TIP: Fill up your water bottles with fresh Hetch Hetchy water.

Left: *Bicyclists and hikers enjoy the scenery at this Greco-Roman temple. Photos courtesy of Tom Wilmer*

Right: *Water is so important in California it deserves a temple.*

Inset: *Locals know to fill up their water bottles with fresh Hetch Hetchy H_2O.*

This is one of only three such temples in the United States. Another is the Sunol Water Temple in the East Bay, designed by architect Willis Polk.

SACRAMENTO'S SECOND CITY

Why is the State Capitol jacked up?

Politicians are often accused of covering things up, but in Sacramento legislators are literally sitting on top of secrets dating back to the 19th century.

1861 marked the largest storm in California history. The American River crashed through levees, carrying away houses, stores, and saloons in Sacramento. Steamboats became rescue vessels, and newly elected Governor Leland Stanford was forced to take a rowboat to his inauguration at the Capitol.

Those who didn't flee to San Francisco spent the next 15 years using a jack system to raise city streets and sidewalks. Sacramento was the first city on the West Coast to attempt such an arduous operation.

On the Sacramento History Museum Underground Tours in Old Town you see how first floors became basements and second floors were suddenly the main entrance. Mark Twain saw some humor in the sunken houses, commenting that it "enables the inquiring stranger to rest his elbows on the second-story windowsill and look in and criticize the bedroom arrangements of the citizens."

After you tour Old Town, drive by a more recent architectural gem known as the Dragon House. Located in a residential area at 2816 22nd St., it's covered in colorful tiles and mosaics with an Asian theme.

Left: *Historic buildings house popular restaurants and boutiques in Sacramento's Old Town.*

Right: *Underground Sacramento is still a digging site for archeologists. Photo courtesy of Sacramento History Museum*

THE CAPITOL'S UNDERWORLD

WHAT: Old Sacramento Underground Tour

WHERE: Sacramento History Museum, 101 I St., Sacramento

COST: $18 for adults, $12 for ages 6–12, free for ages 5 and younger

PRO TIP: The museum is not accessible to cars, so it's a little hard to find. Have your navigation system direct you to the California State Railroad Museum next door.

The area is still an active archeological site, and some of the artifacts they've discovered include: a doll's head, whiskey bottles, gold-rimmed mirrors, a porcelain chamber pot, and toothbrushes miners could rent! On the evening tour guides tell salacious stories about the era's brothels, gambling, and murders.

Just walking around Sacramento, you can see indications of this former underground world: there are sidewalk skylights along J and K streets downtown.

METAMORPHOSIS

How do you shed your cocoon?

Trapeze artists, harpsichordists strumming in a sculpture garden, opera singers bedecked in layers of chiffon and glitter in a mosaic courtyard, monkeys, rabbits, peacocks, and talking parrots . . . they're all part of Metamorphosis, one of the many colorful interactive experiences at the Gregangelo Museum.

Your senses will be overwhelmed as you step into a storybook. It's an incongruous setting, a house in a suburban San Francisco neighborhood, but just as this home has been transformed into a fairyland, you'll find yourself changed by the end of Metamorphosis.

The guides, including a butterfly catcher and the Mad Hatter, ask probing questions as you enter each chapter. What do you feel guilty about? Name a time you wish could go on forever. What are you passionate about? After baring your soul, you perch on a mushroom chair to watch aerial dancers, surrounded by peacocks, perform against a psychedelic background.

It's nothing new for Gregangelo Herrera, the circus ringmaster. He's constantly coming up with new ways to wow an audience. In addition to Metamorphosis, he and his team of performers created Riddle of the Sphinx, an hour-long puzzle in the sculpture gardens.

Gregangelo is nicknamed the whirling dervish for a reason. He's constantly reinventing his surroundings, and

Get a copy of *The Trees of San Francisco* book before your visit. Many rare and unusual species are located in this neighborhood.

WHERE FAIRY TALES COME TRUE

WHAT: Gregangelo Museum

WHERE: 225 San Leandro Way, San Francisco

COST: Depends on the tour

PRO TIP: Bring a jacket for the outdoor tour; this part of town can get chilly even in summer.

Left: *Monkey see monkey do.*

Right: *Acrobats are just part of the entertainment here.*

Inset: *A harpsichordist helps you transform.*

taking a tour of his house is like entering a kaleidoscope, where each room tries to outdo the next with colorful murals, mosaic tiles, and drapes. At any moment you expect Salvador Dalí to greet you.

133

HOLLYWOOD NORTH

Where did Charlie Chaplin get his big break?

There was a time when a Podunk town in the Bay Area gave Tinsel Town a run for its money. In the early 1900s the Essanay Film Studios in Niles churned out hundreds of silent movies in just a few years thanks to Bronco Billy, the first Western movie star.

Following the success of *The Great American Train Robbery*, Billy, aka Gilbert Anderson, began writing and directing his films. While scouting locations he settled on Niles, with canyons perfect for ambushes and a train stop that made it easy to visit the Essanay headquarters in Chicago. Suddenly actors, camera operators, and support staff invaded Niles to work at Essanay Studios' California location.

Anderson's greatest triumph was not making Westerns, but rather signing Charlie Chaplin, a relatively unknown actor. Chaplin filmed five movies in Niles, including *The Tramp*. His movie premieres were in the same place you can see his silent films today, the Edison Theater. Just like 1913, when Chaplin sat in these seats, live piano music accompanies the silent films.

Next door, the Niles Essanay Silent Film Museum displays an honorary Oscar for Bronco Billy, the wooden door from the Essanay film studios (which was destroyed), vintage hand-crank film projectors, original 1920s movie posters, and 10,000 silent films. Every year the Museum holds Charlie Chaplin days where characters in period costumes lead tours.

Ride a vintage train to see where Chaplin filmed *The Tramp*. The Niles Canyon Railway is a living history museum that runs antique trains between Sunol and Niles Canyon.

WHERE SILENCE IS GOLDEN

WHAT: Niles Essanay Silent Film Museum

WHERE: 37417 Niles Blvd., Fremont

COST: The museum is free—donations are requested. The movie screenings are also no cost, but suggested donations are: $7 for Not Members Yet and $5 for members.

PRO TIP: Niles, which is now a part of Fremont, is known for its shops selling collectibles and every August the town holds the Annual Antiques Faire and Flea Market.

Top left: *The former west coast studio for Essanay films.*

Top right: *Charlie Chaplin in* The Tramp.

Center left: *You can see vintage cameras and movie posters at the Essanay film museum.*

Bottom left: *Who knew Fremont was once a movie capital?*

Inset: *Charlie Chaplin not only became a star in Niles, he directed and wrote movies. Photo courtesy of Niles Essanay Silent Film Museum*

The actor couldn't wait to move to Los Angeles, and Niles residents were not sorry to see him go. Reportedly he went under the bleachers during sports events and pinched girls bottoms at a time when women couldn't leave the house without a chaperone.

ROCK STAR

How did a vacant lot become an art project?

Dave Dean got tired of walking by a vacant lot overrun with weeds and trash, so he began cleaning it up. This good deed was noticed by the lot's owners, the city of Encinitas. They sent Dean a cease and desist order, but it didn't deter him. He continued his work after dark. "I was a Ninja gardener," he laughs.

To create pathways Dean collected stones from nearby Moonlight State Beach, and one day a woman painted a black and white heart medallion on one of the rocks. "I said, that's it! I'm going to have a thousand rocks in a thousand colors by a thousand people," exclaims Dean. He began inviting beachgoers to stop for a minute and join him painting rocks.

The goal was to bring people together, says Dean, and now people from 90 different countries, ranging in age from 1 to 100, have painted 7,000 pieces of rock art. "They come from all over: Colombia, Zimbabwe, Scotland, and New Zealand," says Dean, who thinks it may be the most interactive art project in the state. It's a constantly evolving installation with newly adorned rocks added every day.

Walking through the garden you see rocks with the name of the artist's hometown, rocks with messages in various languages, elaborate nature scenes, surfing Buddhas, angels,

Another eccentric attraction in Encinitas are the Boathouses at 726 Third Street. When the Moonlight Beach Dance Pavilion went dark, architect Miles Kellogg used the reclaimed wood to build the SS Moonlight and the SS Encinitas, apartment buildings that resemble ships.

Left: *People come from all over the world to paint a rock and add it to this unusual garden.*

ROCK ON

WHAT: Dave's Rock Garden

WHERE: 200–298 B St., Encinitas

COST: Free

PRO TIP: On Saturdays and Sundays Dean supplies brushes, rocks, and paint, but if you visit another day remember to BYOP, bring your own paint.

Right: *Many people discover the rock garden walking to the Moonlight State Beach.*

Inset: *Sometimes words are the art form on Dave's rocks.*

lots of hearts and peace symbols, and some with funny messages, like "Dear rock, I win—Paper."

The city's support, although rocky in the past, has come full circle. Now Encinitas embraces the garden and even provides free water. "I hose down the rocks every week, but they still don't grow," laughs Dean.

POOL PARTY

Who knows someone with an oceanfront guest home?

Turns out you do! Marion Davies, paramour of William Randolph Hearst, has opened her Santa Monica beach pad to you . . . and everyone else you know.

Apparently a San Simeon castle wasn't enough to keep Davies happy, so Hearst hired Julia Morgan to build a compound along the Santa Monica coastline, nicknamed the Gold Coast. Clark Gable, Carole Lombard, Cary Grant, Gloria Swanson, and Charlie Chaplin all sunbathed, drank champagne, and splashed water at one another in the same tiled pool you can enjoy today.

Over the years, fires, taxes, and earthquakes took their toll, and the 100-room house was demolished. The pool house became a Motor Inn, then the Sand & Sea Club, until finally the city of Santa Monica took it over, but the upkeep on this beachfront estate was daunting. Luckily Wallis Annenberg had fond memories of swimming there as a child, so she enlisted her foundation to help restore the estate. Now the public can enjoy a movie star's life for at least an afternoon.

THE OTHER HEARST CASTLE

WHAT: Annenberg Community Beach House

WHERE: 415 Pacific Coast Hwy., Santa Monica

COST: Free if you walk or bike in, nominal cost for parking and use of the pool.

PRO TIP: If you get tired of lounging by the pool, you can rent paddleboards.

Check out the Camera Obscura in Santa Monica, a device used by Leonardo da Vinci to mimic the human eye. In a dark room you look through a small hole that lets in light, and you can see the outside world.

Top left: *Previously only open to celebrities, today anyone can enjoy the Davies Guest House. Photo courtesy of the Annenberg Community Beach House*

Right: *Every beach house needs a fireplace. Photo courtesy of Kari Bible*

Bottom left: *This is just the guest house, the main home burned down! Photo courtesy of the Annenberg Community Beach House*

Instead of seeing celebrities (although there may be some in the crowd—this is LA after all!), these days you'll see and hear from writers, dancers, and Shakespearean actors at the Beach House's cultural performances. Be sure and sign up for the docent-led tours of public art, including a new mural along the beach walk.

In the Marion Davies Guest House, a five-bed, five-bath home (this was not the main house!), the original Tiffany chandeliers, marble fireplaces, and hardwood floors are still intact. The guesthouse is also rented for private events, everything from weddings to corporate retreats.

SAND CASTLE

How did a castle end up in a beach town?

If surfers looking for the perfect wave and hikers trying to spot whales from the bluffs above Rockaway Beach in Pacifica would only turn around, they would spot something rarer: a medieval fortress.

You'd expect to see Sam's Castle in a European village, but not in the suburban Sharp Park neighborhood about a half hour south of San Francisco. Its concrete turrets, barricades, and battlements were all a reaction to the 1906 earthquake and subsequent fires. Rail magnate Henry McCloskey's house was severely damaged by "the big one," and he was so shook up he built a replica of his wife's childhood home in Scotland that could withstand any disaster—fire, quake, or an invasion of marauding surfers.

Over the years it has been a speakeasy, a brothel, and during World War II a barracks for the Coast Guard—who reportedly trashed the place. Sam Mazza bought it for $29,000 in 1959 but never lived there. Instead, this painter and decorator for lavish theater sets filled the castle with his quirky collection of art and antiques. He used it to hold parties, community events, and fundraisers—including one for McCloskey's grandson Pete. When Republican Pete McCloskey was running for Congress, he wanted to be the first to win Pacifica, a Democratic stronghold. Mazza held a campaign event at the castle, and McCloskey credits it with cinching his victory.

FIT FOR A KING

WHAT: Sam's Castle

WHERE: 900 Mirador Ter., Pacifica

COST: Free

PRO TIP: If you want to learn about the building's rich history, check out Images of America: Sam's Castle by Bridget Oates.

Top: *Sam's Castle was built to withstand any disaster from earthquakes to floods. Photo courtesy of VisitPacifica.com*

Inset: *Who wouldn't feel regal with these views? Photo courtesy of VisitPacifica.com*

When Mazza died the estate was turned over to the Sam Mazza Foundation, which occasionally opens it to the public. If you visit, you'll get the royal treatment. Visitors can sit on the throne in a robe and crown waving a scepter toward the suit of armor.

Nobility naturally needs an archery range, and the city obliges. There are three ranges in Pacifica and they offer free lessons for beginners.

141

FRISCO FRIVOLITY

Where can you be a sailor for the night?

In the 1800s, when the wind died and sailors were stuck at sea, they sang sea chanteys to cure the doldrums. When the world came to a standstill due to COVID, sea chanteys made a comeback. Blimey, TikTok of all places started the trend in 2020.

San Francisco (nicknamed Frisco by sailors) claims the oldest continuous sea chantey sing-along in the world. Shiver me timbers, since 1989 the National Park Service has invited professional musicians and landlubbers alike to perform on historic schooners at the Hyde St. Pier, part of the San Francisco Maritime Historical Park. Well after the sun sets over the yardarm, the sea chanteys, accompanied by water splashing against the planks and creaking wood, echo across the Bay.

This chantey revival is run by the San Francisco Maritime National Historical Park. Park ranger Peter Kasin, who organizes the evenings, says "I was inspired to join the Forest Service after attending a sea chantey event in the '80s." In addition to the sea chantey evenings and

SINGING SAILORS

WHAT: Sea chantey sing-alongs

WHERE: Hyde Street Pier, 2905 Hyde St., San Francisco

COST: Free

PRO TIP: The interactive visitors center in Fisherman's Wharf shows the important role ships played in San Francisco history.

Visit the park's maritime library at Fort Mason to learn more about the ships buried under the city's Financial District. Peruse diaries, logbooks, and historic photos in a room overlooking the Bay.

Top left: *After visiting the Hyde St. Pier make your way to the Maritime Museum in the Aquatic Park Bathhouse building.*

Right: *Fishing, sailing, swimming, are just a few of things you can do at the historic Hyde St. Pier before singing sea chanteys.*

Bottom left: *Warming up to sing sea chanteys on the* Eureka.

Inset: *Walk down the wooden sidewalk to see working fishing boats.*

other musical events on the Pier, the park offers docent tours of the schooners to increase interest in seafaring culture.

San Francisco Maritime National Historical Park is really not a "park" at all but rather a historic neighborhood. It encompasses the historic vessels at Hyde Street Pier; Aquatic Park cove and beach, popular with polar bear swimmers; and the Maritime Museum, located in a Streamline Moderne bathhouse. Recently the museum discovered WPA murals hidden under layers of paint, and restoration experts made them shipshape.

MOTEL MILESTONE

Where is the world's first motel?

In the roaring '20s, Californians were relishing the freedom of the open road thanks to the Ford Model T, or Tin Lizzie, the first affordable car. Previous cars were so expensive that it was a news story when someone bought one, says Thomas Kessler, executive director of the History Center of San Luis Obispo County.

Californians were driving up and down the Pacific coast, and one clever architect, Arthur Heineman, took advantage of the trend, building the first "motor hotel" halfway between San Francisco and Los Angeles. In 1925 the Milestone Mo-Tel Inn (later the Motel Inn) opened in San Luis Obispo.

In a 1926 article, the *Los Angeles Times* explained the new concept: "The motel plan eliminates a long walk through dark streets in a strange town between a garage and a hotel. The motorist's car is where he is, ready for the road for an early morning start." Small garages were located next to the bungalows, with additional rooms for chauffeurs.

During this era California was rejecting East Coast architecture and embracing its Spanish heritage, so the Motel Inn had a Mission Revival style with a red-tile roof and a bell tower modeled after the one atop Santa Barbara's courthouse.

It was an immediate success, and Heineman planned to make it a chain, each motel a day's drive apart. Although the Great Depression ruined his dream, he could take comfort

To learn more about the Mo-Tel and other fascinating facts about the area, visit the History Center of San Luis Obispo County, located in a Carnegie library building across the street from the Mission.

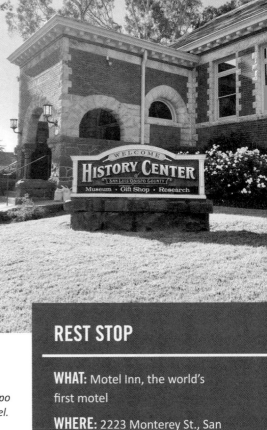

Left: *Marilyn Monroe and Joe DiMaggio stayed here on their honeymoon.*

Right: *The History Center of San Luis Obispo County has more information on the motel.*

REST STOP

WHAT: Motel Inn, the world's first motel

WHERE: 2223 Monterey St., San Luis Obispo

COST: Free

PRO TIP: As befits the first motel, it is not easy to get there any way but via an automobile.

in the famous guests that stayed here, including Marilyn Monroe and Joe DiMaggio, who had lunch here during their honeymoon. Heineman was clearly ahead of his time. The word "motel" did not appear in a dictionary until 1950, 25 years after the Milestone opened.

Today all that remains are the sign and the building's facade. Rumors persist of developers re-opening the motel, but so far nothing has materialized.

FROM RUSSIA WITH LOVE

Why is a musical about a California woman popular in Russia?

Ah, the great tragic love stories . . . Romeo and Juliet, Heathcliff and Cathy, and Conchita and Nikolai.

Never heard of the last one? In Russia it inspired a ballad, a novel, and a hit musical, *Juno and Avos*, as popular there as *Jesus Christ Superstar* is here.

The great romance for the ages began in 1806 at the San Francisco Presidio Officers Club, which is still standing. Russian explorer Nikolai Petrovich Rezanov was in town getting supplies after sailing the *Juno and Avos* from a fur-trading settlement in Alaska. At a reception in his honor Rezanov met Concepcion (nicknamed Conchita) Arguello, daughter of the Presidio comandante Don Jose Dario Arguello.

In his journal, the ship's doctor wrote glowingly of Conchita: she was vivacious, with brilliant eyes, exceedingly beautiful teeth, and a shapely figure. Nikolai and Conchita fell in love despite their many challenges, including geographical distance, religious and cultural differences, a language barrier, and a wide gap in their ages—Conchita was 15, and he was 42!

Nevertheless they were determined to marry, and Rezanov left San Francisco to get permission from the czar for the union. As time went by with no word from her

DOOMED ROMANCE

WHAT: Grave of Concepcion Arguello

WHERE: St. Dominic's Cemetery, East Fifth Street and Hillcrest Avenue, Benicia. Her grave is on the left as you enter.

COST: Free

PRO TIP: If you can't get to Benecia, the star-crossed lovers are immortalized in a mural on the inside walls of the Presidio of San Francisco chapel.

Left: At the entrance to St. Dominic's cemetery in Benicia there is a monument to Concepcion Arguello.

Top center: Benicia is also home to Robert Arneson's artistic surf board bench.

Bottom center: Told you not to look under here!

Right: At the Presidio Chapel a mural includes Concepcion Arguello with Nikolai Petrovich Rezanov.

fiancé, Concepcion waited patiently, refusing many suitors. After five years, one of his officers visited Concepcion to return the locket she had given Rezanov. He died falling off his horse, and reportedly his last words were about Conchita.

Inconsolable, Concepcion joined a Dominican convent in Benicia, where legend has it she wrote California's first textbook. Her memorial in St. Dominic's Cemetery in Benicia is a popular stop for Russian visitors, who often leave behind soil from Rezanov's grave.

Benicia is known as an artists' colony, and there are lots of outdoor art installations to enjoy, including a bench by Robert Arneson at the marina. Be sure to look underneath for a secret message.

CHEERIO

What's a double-decker bus doing on the California coast?

If you're feeling a bit peckish and pining for a pint of lager, you needn't cross the pond. Cameron's Pub in Half Moon Bay has bangers and mash, a red British phone booth, and a store stocked with English goods that will make you chuffed to bits.

TASTE OF BRITAIN

WHAT: Cameron's Pub

WHERE: 1410 S Cabrillo Hwy., Half Moon Bay

COST: Free to look, moderate prices on food and beverages

PRO TIP: Avoid Half Moon Bay near Halloween. The city holds an annual pumpkin festival that stops traffic for miles.

Driving down Highway 1 you can't miss it . . . just look for the red double-decker bus. It gets the attention of drivers, laughs owner Cameron Palmer, who claims it's the only double-decker smoking bus. When the California smoking ban went into effect in 1997, he declared the bus a designated smoking area and installed TVs for sports fans.

Before the Cameron's Pub sign was installed 30 years ago, the building was a brothel, murder scene, and—legend has it—slot machine operation for Al Capone's sister. "Half Moon Bay was the other side of the world back then," says Palmer, "and the coast was a bootlegging mecca. Ships dumped barrels of whiskey in the water and let the waves carry them to the beach."

Although Palmer was born in San Francisco, he understands pubs. His father hails from Newcastle, and he has numerous relatives in England.

Customers love photo ops in front of the phone booth, trolley car, and a stock and pillory. Popular menu items include fish and chips and homemade English pasties. A small British import shop has groceries difficult to find in the United States. There's also a jolly good game room with darts and

148

Top left: *The red double-decker bus makes it easy to spot Cameron's Pub.*

Top right: *Cameron's extensive collection of beer cans is on display behind the bar.*

Bottom: *Visitors have lots of options for staying overnight, camping, a hotel, and the Pub's B&B. Photos courtesy of Jeff Broyles*

shuffleboard, and if you get knackered there's a B&B upstairs, but it stands for bed and beverage—no breakfast.

The website proclaims it's "a place where babies and grandmums are welcome," and "If you can't find a beer you like, you must not like beer."

See world-class jazz musicians in an intimate setting at the Douglas Beach House on Miramar Beach. The Bach Dancing and Dynamite Society has hosted Sunday afternoon concerts here since 1964.

TRUTH SEEKERS' SANCTUARY

What is the meaning of life?

California has always been an open place that looks to the esoteric and occult to solve modern-day problems. So it's no surprise it embraced Manly Hall, author of *An Encyclopedic Outline of Masonic, Hermetic, Qabbalistic and Rosicrucian Symbolical Philosophy*, more commonly known as *The Secret Teachings of All Ages*. A trip around the world provided inspiration for his lavishly illustrated, massive tome that covers secret societies, arcane practices, mythology, symbolism, and astrology.

After its success Hall created The Philosophical Research Society or PRS in 1935. Hidden in the Los Feliz neighborhood of Los Angeles, it looks like a bland cement apartment building from the outside. Once you enter the Mayan-style courtyard overflowing with bougainvillea, however, it becomes a quiet refuge from the busy city. The library contains manuscripts of all beliefs from Aristotle to the Freemasons. It's so inclusive that during World War II, The Library of Congress requested permission to make microfilm copies of unique items for a permanent record, in case the library was bombed.

You may recognize the exquisite wood-paneled, two-story library with moving wooden lecterns from TV shows and

---

Nearby Griffith Park has the remnants of the original LA Zoo. When the zoo relocated, it left behind cages and stone exhibits, and the ruins have been turned into a picnic area.

Left: *PRS is often used for movies and TV show settings.*

Right: *Mayan architecture invites guests to the courtyard.*

movies. It's also popular with location scouts, as well as writers researching period films. Hall himself dabbled in the movies, writing a murder mystery movie, *When Were You Born*, in which astrology was used to find the killer. Hall, who was reportedly good friends with Bela Lugosi, made a cameo appearance in this camp film.

In addition to the library, PRS offers online classes, holds lectures and movie screenings in a small auditorium, and there's a bookstore.

A WISE CHOICE

WHAT: The Philosophical Research Society

WHERE: 3910 Los Feliz Blvd., Los Angeles

COST: Free

PRO TIP: You can't bring food or drink into the library, so grab a bite beforehand in one of the wooden booths at the nearby Little Dom's Italian restaurant.

CIRCUS CEMETERY

Where do show folks go when the carnival closes?

A barrel of fun at a cemetery? Yep, if you visit the Circus monument in the Olivet Memorial Park in Colma. Dedicated to the Show Folks of America, this stone monument is colorfully decorated with a brightly painted clown, dubbed the "clown of eternal jest," laughing under the Big Top and surrounded by a Ferris wheel, merry-go-round and other amusement rides. The monument, inscribed with the words, "That they may rest in peace among their own," is adjacent to plots called "Showman's rest."

On occasion the Show Folks of America erect a big top here to celebrate their colleagues' lives and place flags on the gravestones. In 1945 the group decided to buy 600 plots after a member jumped off the Golden Gate Bridge and no one would bury him, says Marta Quinn, Show Folks of America treasurer, who adds the organization has a savings account for those who can't afford a burial. Today more than 200 members are buried in Colma's Clown Alley and the cremated remains of Show Folks are enclosed inside the monument.

CLOWNING AROUND

WHAT: Show Folks of America Memorial

WHERE: 1601 Hillside Blvd., Colma

COST: Free

PRO TIP: The front office of Olivet Memorial Park has maps of the cemetery.

Across the street the most popular items in the Colma History Museum's gift shop have the slogan, "It's great to be alive in Colma."

Left: *"That they may rest in peace with their own"* is inscribed on the crypt.

Right: *Colma is called The City of Souls.*

Inset: *You didn't expect the circus to have a boring monument, did you?*

"We're like a big family. We all know each other," says Quinn. Primarily a social club, it began in San Francisco and is now located in Lodi, California. Members include circus performers, amusement park and carnival employees, ringmasters, tightrope walkers, magicians, jugglers, animal trainers, barkers, game and ride operators, and managers.

Colma is filled with cemeteries and is often called the city of souls, with more dead people than alive. In the early 1900s San Francisco needed land, so it relocated graves here, which is why it is the final resting place for many famous SF residents, including Joe DiMaggio, Emperor Norton, and Wyatt Earp.

DOO DOO DILEMMA

Why is a San Jose art installation controversial?

What happens when a famous artist creates an outdoor art installation that many people confuse for a large animal dropping? It's an ongoing saga in San Jose, with so much gossip and intrigue it could be the top story on *Entertainment Tonight*.

It all started in 1988, when Mayor Tom McEnery convinced the city to erect a statue of Thomas Fallon, the 10th mayor of San Jose. In 1846 Fallon raised an American flag over San Jose after the United States declared war on Mexico. Many opposed the statue claiming Fallon committed atrocities against indigenous people.

In response to the outcry the city commissioned artist Robert Graham to erect a statue celebrating city's Hispanic heritage. Born in Mexico, Graham moved to San Jose when he was 11, studied art at San Jose State, and went on to became a world-renowned sculptor. Along the way he married actor Anjelica Huston.

Graham presented a drawing of the winged serpent Aztec god Quetzalcoatl standing on a pedestal, allowing people to walk inside. This was rejected for fear the unhoused would camp there. Frustrated, Graham went to Mexico for inspiration and came back with a different representation of Quetzalcoatl, a squat, black, coiled snake. Unveiled in 1996, it was met with laughter and shock. Some say this was Graham's revenge for an earlier commission the city rejected, gateways to the city's entrances.

The first museum in the United States to devote itself to this artform, the San Jose Museum of Quilts and Textiles has topical talks such as "Social Justice Sewing."

Robert Graham's unusual sculpture in downtown San Jose surprised the city.

ONE MAN'S TRASH...

WHAT: Quetzalcoatl statue

WHERE: Plaza de Cesar Chavez, 194 S Market St., San Jose

COST: Free

PRO TIP: Other critically acclaimed Graham statues include the celestial women in front of the federal building on First Street.

The city council has since voted to remove the Fallon image, and during discussions of the controversial Christopher Columbus sculpture, one lawmaker said she was prouder of that statue than the one that "looks like a turd."

SCANDINAVIAN STYLE

Why is the Norwegian flag flying on Russian Hill?

Divine inspiration must be easier at a church with one of the best views in San Francisco. From the deck of the Norwegian Seamen's Church, parishioners can see Fisherman's Wharf, Aquatic Park, and the Golden Gate Bridge. This place of worship also goes by the names Church by the Golden Gate and Norway on the Hill.

A white neoclassical mansion, it was reportedly sold for half price when the owners learned it would become a church. Norwegians had a good reputation in San Francisco. At the dedication ceremony in 1951, Mayor Elmer Robinson noted that he seldom had to deal with criminals of Norwegian heritage because "they are law-abiding citizens."

Like the rest of the world, Norwegians flocked to San Francisco during the gold rush, and their maritime skills guaranteed them jobs if they didn't make their fortune in mining. One of the most famous expats was Peder Sather, a banker, who was a trustee of the College of California (now UC Berkeley). His widow funded the construction of the UCB's Sather Gate and Campanile in his honor.

Tourists walking by the church on their way to Fisherman's Wharf usually notice the large anchor in the yard and the Norwegian and Swedish flags blowing in the ever-present wind. Few realize they can come inside, relax on the balcony

Grab a cable car to the Buena Vista Café—famous for its Irish coffee—and gaze on schooners similar to the ones the Norwegians sailed to reach San Francisco.

Left: *The church has views of Alcatraz and Ghirardelli Square.*

Right: *The Norwegian Seaman's Church atop Russian Hill is open to everyone.*

NORWAY ON THE HILL

WHAT: Norwegian Seamen's Church

WHERE: 2454 Hyde St., San Francisco

COST: Free

PRO TIP: Get a selfie with the most photographed Norwegian flag in the world.

overlooking the Bay, and visit the tiny grocery store stocked with Scandinavian treats. Each winter the church holds a Norwegian Christmas Bazaar selling fisherman's wool sweaters, hand-made ornaments, open-face smoked salmon sandwiches, and homemade cakes.

FUSCHIA FUN

Why is San Luis Obispo tickled pink?

No need to wear rose-colored glasses at the Madonna Inn in San Luis Obispo . . . you'll be in the pink from the minute you drive past the fuchsia stagecoach sign.

Everything is rosy here, from the tennis courts to the garbage cans. A swirling signature rose carpet leads guests to a steak house. Pink leather booths, illuminated by dripping chandeliers may compel diners to raise their pinkies. The bakery next door is famous for pink champagne cake adorned with so many curlicues you might mistake it for a fancy 1950s hat.

Built in 1958, this is Barbie's dream hotel. You expect to see Elvis and Liberace by the pool enjoying pink champagne ice cream under blush umbrellas.

The cotton candy theme was, surprisingly, a man's idea. Alex Madonna thought the color was fun. He and his wife, Phyllis, built the Swiss chalet-style hotel into the side of a cliff on a 1,000-acre ranch.

Boulders were used to construct the 110 rooms and each one is unique, so if you have the time and the money you can play Goldilocks. Some of the favorites are Bridal Falls (inspired by Yosemite's Bridalveil waterfall), Barrel of Fun (with a rock fireplace and chairs made out of barrels), What's Left (designed with remnants of carpet, wallpaper, and fabric), and the infamous Caveman room, named Flintstone until Hanna-

---

While in San Luis Obispo, visit Bubblegum Alley, 733 Higuera Street. People from all over the world stick their used gum on these walls downtown, often writing messages. If you forgot to bring your own, there's a gumball machine at the entrance.

Left: *Of course the pool with a view of the city has pink umbrellas.*

Right: *Be sure to order pink champagne along with their signature pink champagne cake at the pink counter.*

Inset: *Keep the rosy theme going by sticking pink gum on Bubblegum Alley. Don't worry, the walls are regularly washed down.*

RETURN TO THE STONE AGE

WHAT: The Madonna Inn

WHERE: 100 Madonna Rd., San Luis Obispo

COST: Free to look; various rates for rooms and meals

PRO TIP: The men's urinal on the bottom floor is infamous. It's a rock waterfall created by Hollywood set designer Harvey Allen Warren.

Barbera sued. The moniker changed, but the Stone Age clubs and animal prints remain. Yabba dabba do!

The Madonna Inn has been immortalized in the art house movie *Aria*, a song by "Weird Al" Yankovic, and most recently TV's *The Bachelor.*

SEEING RED

How can you visit Russia without leaving California?

If watching Elle Fanning play Empress Catherine in The Great whetted your appetite for all things Russian, San Francisco has you covered. The Museum of Russian Culture is dedicated to life before the Bolshevik Revolution in 1917.

It's a nostalgic look at life before communism, with gold-framed photos of the nobility, gold-braided uniforms, and gold-rimmed china. The requisite furry hats are on display alongside vintage advertisements, jewelry, an array of medals, and even toys.

A few of the most significant exhibits include a rug owned by the exiled Romanov family and an Ampex tape recorder, made by Alexander Matveevich Poniatoff's company. The name combines his initials with an ex for excellence. Ampex engineers created the world's first commercially successful videotape recorder in 1956.

The museum is housed in The Russian Center of San Francisco, a 1911 Neo-Baroque building with a ballroom and theater that showcase Russian opera, theater, and folk dancing. The Center also has an impressive library frequented by Russian scholars. Each year the Center hosts a Russian festival with music, dancing, and vodka tasting.

It's a surprise to most locals that there's a vibrant Russian community in the city, primarily along Geary Street in the Avenues. Here you can find the gold-domed Holy

On Russian Hill, reportedly named for Russian sailors who saved lives during the 1906 earthquake, the Holy Trinity Orthodox Cathedral has bells that were donated by Tsar Alexander III.

ROYAL RUSSIA

WHAT: Museum of Russian Culture

WHERE: 2450 Sutter St., San Francisco

COST: Free

PRO TIP: Every February the Center organizes a Russian Festival, where you can eat piroshki, sample vodkas, and learn traditional folk dances.

Left: *Russian operas and dances often take place in this neo baroque ballroom and theater.*

Right: *The museum displays pre-revolution military uniforms.*

Inset: *Those who fled Russia during the revolution donated artifacts to the SF museum.*

Virgin Cathedral and a Russian Orthodox church deemed a San Francisco landmark, along with the Red Tavern, and the Russian Renaissance restaurant.

SHADY BUSINESS

Why does California have an underground resort?

Some people, like Baldassare Forestiere, are such visionaries they're not recognized until long after they're dead.

In the early 1900s this Sicilian immigrant began building a subterranean home to escape Fresno's 115-degree summers. Using just a pickax and shovel, over 40 years he created a cool and serene underground mansion, much like Italy's wine cellars. Forestiere used knowledge from his first job in America, digging subways in Boston, to construct arches leading to courtyards with recessed concrete benches, a chapel, a grotto, and even a fishing pond! Leftover materials from his day jobs in construction were used to reinforce the structure.

Skylights provided natural light, allowing citrus trees and grapevines to thrive. When he was above ground, Forestiere loved to lean over and pick fruit. This was all accomplished without any engineering or architectural training, just an

MAN CAVE

WHAT: Forestiere Underground Gardens

WHERE: 5021 W Shaw Ave., Fresno

COST: $21 for adults, $11 for children ages 5–17, free for children 4 and under

PRO TIP: If you visit in summer, go early in the day to stay cool. The gardens are cool but not air conditioned.

For more inspiration, visit Fresno's Starving Artists Bistro. It has an open mic to promote local performers and musicians, and the walls feature artwork by rising stars.

Left: *The Forestiere home doesn't need air conditioning; it's cool even in hot Fresno summers.*

Right: *Forestiere could walk along the perimeter of his home and pick fresh fruit.*

Inset: *The birds were the only ones who could see him bathing in his outdoor bathtub.*

intuitive sense of design. At the time people thought he was crazy, but today acclaimed architects in Spain and Australia are copying him, building homes partially underground.

Forestiere had big plans to open a resort, guessing the cool temperatures underground would attract locals during hot summer months. He constructed a ballroom, an aquarium, and an auto tunnel before he died. His relatives sold off some of the land then, but thanks to his brother, who lived nearby, the main house was preserved. Forestiere is now a historical landmark so everyone can appreciate this architectural marvel.

PRESIDENTIAL PENTHOUSE

What is the most expensive hotel room in San Francisco?

The Fairmont San Francisco is legendary for many reasons: architect Julia Morgan designed the building, it's where Tony Bennett debuted "I Left My Heart in San Francisco," and it was the first hotel to offer concierge services.

But most people don't know about the 6,000-square-foot penthouse that takes up the entire eighth floor. This is where Elton John played the grand piano, Mick Jagger had a wild party, and JFK snuck Marilyn Monroe out a secret door when Jackie made a surprise visit. Marlene Dietrich, Prince Charles, Nat King Cole, Bill Clinton, and Barack Obama have all enjoyed the suite's private deck with a stunning skyline view. In 1945, President Truman met with world leaders at the dining room table, which seats 60, to draft the Charter of the United Nations.

Credit the roaring '20s with the suite's opulence. John Drum, a local businessman, convinced the hotel to let him live there for $1,000 a month when the going rate for other suites was $10 a night. Drum hired Arthur Upham Pope, an archaeologist, UC Berkeley professor, and expert on Persian art, to decorate. His touches include a hand-painted map of the world in the children's bedroom and a billiards room covered from floor to vaulted ceiling in hand-painted

STARRY NIGHTS

WHAT: Fairmont San Francisco penthouse suite

WHERE: 950 Mason St., San Francisco

COST: $18,000 a night, or request a free tour

PRO TIP: Stop by the hotel's Tonga Room & Hurricane Bar, which has indoor thunderstorms and umbrella drinks.

Left: *Check out the books in the penthouse library, including* Secret San Francisco: a Guide to the Weird, Wonderful, and Obscure.

Top right: *Movie stars and presidents have enjoyed the view from the penthouse. Photo courtesy of the Fairmont Hotel*

Bottom right: *An archeologist decorated the Penthouse. Photo courtesy of the Fairmont Hotel*

yellow, purple, and turquoise tiles. A red circular stairway leads to the second floor of the library, which has a gold leaf hand-painted celestial dome ceiling. One of the bookshelves hides a secret door reportedly used by diplomats and "the Blonde Bombshell."

Since 1981 the floor has been available for the mere sum of $18,000 a night. It's also appeared on the TV show *Ballers* and used for an infamous balcony scene with Nicolas Cage and Sean Connery in *The Rock* movie.

Good news for those who can't afford the penthouse: anyone can visit the Fairmont's dog-friendly rooftop garden.

SURF ART

Why are people decorating a statue every day?

Locals love to hate the surfer statue at Cardiff by the Sea. Magic Carpet Ride, better known as the Cardiff Kook, was created by sculptor Matthew Antichevich, who was attempting to recreate his experience as a beginner surfer at Cardiff.

Surfers, who felt the pose was laughable, nicknamed it the Cardiff Kook, and they've been trying to improve his look ever since. Under cover of night, mostly anonymous "artists" have created elaborate costumes—Spiderman, Vincent van Gogh, and a great white shark eating the statue. It's so popular there is a Cardiff Kook calendar featuring his various incarnations.

The sculpture was commissioned by Encinitas, the city next door, and Jim Gilliam, the arts administrator, says these are technically acts of vandalism. Mayor Catherine Blakespear, however, says the statue makeovers are now part of the city's culture.

"It's an icon in this part of northern coastal San Diego County," says Blakespear, who lives in Cardiff by the Sea. And not just this area. When Blakespear was traveling abroad, she saw a photo of the Cardiff Kook. "I'm proud to have the Cardiff Kook in our city, and I love the different costumes. Some of the craftsmanship is very high level. Hours were spent creating these unusual and creative works." One of

Talk about the Kook at Neptune's Portal, a large green cylinder with a hidden video camera at 678 Neptune Avenue. The artist, who calls it a passageway between the past and the future, posts the messages online.

Left: *You never know what the Cardiff Kook will be wearing!*

Right: *The statue is a popular place to celebrate birthdays. Photo courtesy of Jennifer Van Voorst*

HANG 10 OR HANG WHATEVER YOU WANT

WHAT: Cardiff Kook surfing statue

WHERE: S Coast Highway at Chesterfield Dr., Encinitas

COST: Free

PRO TIP: The city of Encinitas has a guided downtown walking tour that includes surf culture.

her favorite things about the statue: "If you're sitting at the light on Chesterfield Street, the Kook is literally riding the wave. It's where the ocean meets the horizon—a cool visual effect."

The Kook has become the unofficial town square, says Blakespear, where people gather for events like a recent Black Lives Matter rally.

ZZYZX

What community is known for the Hollywood Pep Cocktail?

California's public university system is world renowned, so it's surprising to learn that it operates a research center in a place called Zzyzx, where streets have names like Boulevard of Dreams.

Zzyzx (pronounced zye-zix—rhymes with rye-six) was a mineral springs and health resort in the 1940s, established by a huckster who said his spa was the last name in health. "Dr." Curtis Springer (he left school after the ninth grade) broadcast his popular radio show from here, hawking products such as Hollywood Pep Cocktail and Nerve Cell Food. He sold so many of his "cures" that the nearby town of Baker had to build a post office to accommodate his mail.

The resort was successful until Springer's lies caught up with him and the "King of Quack," as the American Medical Association called him, went to jail. The Bureau of Land Management, which owned the property, then turned it over to the California State University Desert Studies Center.

The name and quirky history aren't the only unusual things about Zzyzx. In the middle of the desert, it's truly an oasis, with beautiful Lake Tuendae surrounded by palm trees. This unique ecosystem in the Mojave National Preserve has attracted biologists, geologists, archaeologists, climatologists, and astronomers. David Attenborough filmed a documentary

THE LAST WORD IN DESERT RESEARCH

WHAT: CSU Desert Studies Center

WHERE: Zzyzx in the Mojave National Preserve

COST: Nominal for education groups

PRO TIP: The notorious and secret fraternal organization E Clampus Vitus posted a historical marker near the entrance to Zzyzx.

Top: *Sundown in the desert. Photo courtesy of National Park Service*

Bottom left and right: *Scientists study the wildlife in Zzyzx. Photos courtesy of Jason Wallace*

here, it was the testing ground for a Mars rover, and the state conducted studies on how high-speed rail would affect the resident bighorn sheep.

The center welcomes education and research groups, but reservations are mandatory.

Visit a lava tube in the Mojave National Preserve. Formed by molten lava, they are now underground shelters from the heat, with great photography opportunities.

THORNBURG VILLAGE

Where can you live happily ever after?

Berkeley—or Berserkeley as locals call it—is known for its radical new-age ideas. So it's surprising to learn that one hidden neighborhood is dedicated to the past.

Thornburg Village is an enchanting group of homes straight out of a fairytale. You expect to see turrets, towers, gables, gargoyles, thatch roofs, coats of arms, courtyards, and winding stone stairways in rural Europe, not on a suburban street close to the UC Berkeley campus.

The neighborhood is named after the developer, Jack Thornburg, who was in his 20s when he planned this storybook apartment complex. Where others saw devastation following a 1923 wildfire that destroyed 600 homes, he saw opportunity. Initially Thornburg wanted retail and grocery stores in the same development, but it was forbidden by city zoning laws.

URBAN VILLAGE

WHAT: Thornburg Village

WHERE: 1781–1851 Spruce St., Berkeley

COST: Free to explore

PRO TIP: This is a popular spot for wedding photos, so if you visit on the weekend, you may spot a happy couple.

For contemporary architecture in Berkeley, check out the Fish House at 2747 Mathews Street. In the 1990s, Eugene Tsui designed this concrete home, resembling a sea creature, to withstand any natural disaster.

Left: *You'll swear you're in Europe in this Berkeley neighborhood.*

Right: *History and literature students at the nearby UC campus will feel as though they've entered their textbooks in Thornburg Village.*

William Yelland, the architect, influenced by his time in France during WWI, was partial to this style. His other medieval buildings include the landmark downtown Tupper and Reed Building, known for a jaunty iron pied piper atop the chimney.

Much like his village, Thornburg had a charmed life. After this project he left real estate and became a pilot. He flew rescue missions to Japan during World War II, was one of the first TWA pilots, and taught Barry Goldwater how to fly.

Thornburg Village appears to remain magical. Residents rarely leave, and there is intense competition for the occasional vacancy in this captivating neighborhood.

BOLINAS BUBBLE

What town outlawed road signs?

California beach towns; Santa Monica, Santa Cruz, Santa Barbara, and San Diego to name a few, invest heavily in marketing campaigns encouraging tourists to spend their discretionary money on restaurants, hotels, and attractions. But one unincorporated beach town about an hour from San Francisco doesn't want any visitors. They're so adamant about remaining isolated they remove road signs as soon as they're installed by the Department of Motor Vehicles.

Residents of tiny Bolinas, called Bo by locals, want to keep their idyllic hamlet along the coast all to themselves. Thanks to its location, accessible only by winding country roads with hairpin turns, and water restrictions, large scale development is not feasible.

But in this age of social media, it's impossible to keep anything a secret. Movie stars and tech moguls have moved in next to surfers, hippies, and artists, and you'll see them all walking to the beach, drinking at Smiley's Schooner Saloon, dining at one of the few restaurants, shopping at the honor system produce stand, and listening to impromptu concerts from anyone who feels like playing the community piano located in a downtown courtyard.

This self-imposed isolation was beneficial during the pandemic. Wealthy locals paid to provide free COVID testing for all residents and workers. Tourists trying to escape the city and visit Bolinas were met at the entrance by locals holding up signs saying "Go Home." The small size of the city and early

---

THE UNCONVENTIONAL BEACH TOWN

WHAT: Bolinas

WHERE: About an hour northwest of San Francisco in Marin County

COST: Free to visit

PRO TIP: Smiley's just added a small hotel, one of the few options for staying overnight here.

Left: *These are the only signs you'll find in Bolinas. As soon as officials place directional signs, they're torn down.*

Right: *Can you blame Bolinas for wanting to keep paradise to themselves?*

Inset: *This artists's colony has been discovered by movie stars and techies.*

testing meant that Bolinas was one of a handful of cities around the world with few if any COVID infections, according to a study by the University of California, San Francisco. Sounds like Bolinas is on to something.

Nearby Stinson Beach, which welcomes visitors, has one of the best swimming spots in Northern California. If swimming isn't enough exercise, hikers can take the Dipsea Trail through Muir Woods to this white sand beach.

SUSPENSEFUL SAN DIEGO

Where do swingers hang out in San Diego?

In the early 1900s, a visionary mayor named Edwin Capps was instrumental in transforming the San Diego Harbor into a major seaport and convincing the city to invest in tourism rather than factories. One of his lesser-known achievements though was created for locals: the Spruce Street Suspension Bridge.

An engineer, Capps designed this footbridge across a canyon so Bankers Hill residents could reach the new trolley car line. Today the streetcars are history, but the bridge still amazes children, inspires romantics, and delights nature lovers. Just a few minutes from downtown San Diego, it's a tranquil retreat from the tourist throngs.

Walking across the swaying wooden planks with a view of the downtown skyline feels as though you're floating in the treetops. The canyon below the bridge is named after Kate Sessions, a horticulturist responsible for planting trees and bushes around the city.

The "wiggly bridge" is supported by concrete piers anchored to steel suspension cables. Those who are skittish should be

SWAY WITH IT

WHAT: Suspension bridge

WHERE: 220 Spruce St., San Diego

COST: Free

PRO TIP: The bridge is closed from 10 p.m. to 6 a.m.

See more of San Diego horticulture at Harper's Topiary Garden, 3549 Union Street. A yard sign says "Edna Scissorhands" transforms the hedges into life-size figurines, including a rabbit, whale, and cowboy.

Left: *The Suspension Bridge sways over a forest not far from downtown San Diego.*

Right: *The Bridge was originally built to help residents reach a trolley line.*

Inset: *Rollerbladers, skateboarders and walkers all enjoy the bridge.*

aware it has the capacity to hold thousands of walkers and is routinely inspected.

Although Capps was a popular mayor, elected twice, he was not without his controversies. During a record drought he hired a rainmaker. Charles Hatfield was successful—so successful that the showers led to deadly flooding. It's said he inspired the Rainmaker film starring Burt Lancaster and Katharine Hepburn.

TOAD TUNNEL

Why did Davis build a town for amphibians?

Mr. Toad's Wild Ride was never as scary as the journey toads in Davis once traveled. That's what city leaders thought, anyway.

Frogs and toads happily hopped from one side of a dirt lot to a reservoir until the city decided to replace the dirt with the Pole Line Road overpass in 1995. Incensed animal activists said the toads would be cut off from ancestral wetlands and many would become roadkill. Before you could say ribbit the town built a toad tunnel to help them travel safely, and it cost anywhere from $5,000 to $30,000 depending on whom you ask.

A tunnel may have saved their lives, but the good people of Davis thought it didn't go far enough for their jumpy friends. Ted Puntillo Sr., the former postmaster, built a miniature village at the end of the tunnel, near the post office. Toad Hollow includes a tiny hotel, saloon, outhouse, and fountain, with cartoon frogs painted on the windows. Then Puntillo made his froggy friends immortal by writing a children's book, *The Toads of Davis: A Saga of a Small Town*.

This got the attention of the Daily Show, which installed a camera to see how many toads used the tunnel. "There were no leaping frogs while they recorded and . . . we've never proven toads use it, but according to some, they psychically know we did this for them," says Bob Bowen, retired city spokesperson.

In Davis, those who can't jump, bike. So it's only fitting that the unofficial bike capital of the nation is home to the United States Bicycling Hall of Fame.

A CITY OF TOADYS

WHAT: Toad Hollow

WHERE: 2020 Fifth St., Davis

COST: Free

PRO TIP: You're more likely to see frogs in the UC Davis arboretum.

Top left: *Next to the post office an entire toad town was built.*

Center left: *In addition to tunnels for toads, turkeys have the right of way in Davis.*

Right: *Toads—who doesn't love them?*

Bottom left: *You are more likely to see frogs on the beautiful UC Davis campus. Photo courtesy of University of California, Davis*

Whether the toads were appreciative or not, the city has embraced them. There is a Mr. Toad mascot, a street and dog park are named after them, and so far, no reports of warts.

Protecting amphibians seems natural when you realize UC Davis began in the early 1900s as the University Farm, an agricultural branch of the University of California system. It wasn't until 1959 that it became the seventh campus.

CITY CAMPING

How do you sleep under the stars when you're an urbanite?

The next time you feel the need to reconnect with nature, don't bother driving to Yosemite or Tahoe—pitch a tent in San Francisco. That's right . . . the city has campgrounds!

Rob Hill, in the Presidio of San Francisco, is an effort to bring a national park experience to an urban area, says Aricia Martinez, visitor services coordinator. It's located just above Baker Beach, where campers can smell the Pacific Ocean, hear the foghorns, and at the same time use their cell phones to order dinner from food delivery apps.

This is the Presidio's highest point, and in 1852 the Army planned to build a small fort or "redoubt" here to spot incoming ships. It was never constructed, but the name Rob Hill was derived from the survey marker reading Redoubt, Telegraph Hill.

Because it's one of the largest campgrounds, allowing 30 people at each site, bookings may include youth groups, classrooms, family reunions, or soccer teams. Sometimes, though, there's still not enough space . . . like the time Martinez had to turn away a parent who wanted to hire an exotic animal petting zoo, including a boa constrictor, for their child's birthday party. It's also popular with hardcore campers, who backpack or bike from the Bay Area Ridge Trail or campgrounds in the Marin Headlands.

Take a hike along the Presidio's new trails, the Tennessee Hollow Watershed Walk and the Quartermaster Reach Marsh. You'll spot a variety of wildlife, including more than 300 species of birds.

Top: *Who says you can't camp out in the middle of the city? You won't hear anything but foghorns at The Presidio.*

Inset: *If you forget the ingredients for s'mores you're in luck . . . city grocery stores are minutes away. Photos courtesy of The Presidio Trust*

URBAN WILDERNESS

WHAT: Rob Hill Campground

WHERE: Presidio; 1475 Central Magazine Rd., San Francisco

COST: $75 to $100 per night, per site

PRO TIP: The campsite is very popular, so make your reservation far in advance.

All the sites have food storage lockers to prevent wildlife interactions, although Martinez says coyotes usually run away when they see people. Rob Hill, open from April 1 to October 31, has parking spaces, and most importantly, indoor toilets! Until 2018 it was the only campground in San Francisco, but now Candlestick Point State Recreation Area also welcomes campers.

WHAT A GAS!

When are ads considered artwork?

Forty years ago, when neon signs were being removed from old buildings and thrown in the trash, two young artists decided to save as many as possible. Lili Lakich and Richard Jenkins (who was still in high school!) wound up with so many signs they created a museum to showcase their electric art.

MONA, the Museum of Neon Art, claims to be the first neon museum in the world and the only museum devoted exclusively to electric art. "The signs were dying out when the museum was founded," says Corrie Siegel, executive director. "Now there's a resurgence of neon as an art form. People are longing for what is real and handmade. There's a magic to the glow and history of neon."

Neon signs were so commonplace in cities that people didn't realize they were built by hand, says Siegel. "All of these signs are built by skilled artisans who spent years training," she says. "It's similar to glassblowing, but more complicated and even though it's commercial, it's still artwork."

You can watch artists fabricating neon tubes at MONA and learn how to make your own electric art. Begin with Bend, Blow and Glow, an introductory class on cutting, welding, and bending glass tubing.

ELECTRIC ATTITUDE

WHAT: MONA, the Museum of Neon Art

WHERE: 216 S Brand Blvd., Glendale

COST: $10

PRO TIP: Contrary to popular belief, Siegel says, people do walk in Los Angeles, and MONA sponsors walking tours of neon art throughout the city.

Left: *Neon ads began to attract passing motorists, and they're making a comeback.*

Right: *Jump right into Hollywood history at the first neon museum in the world.*

Inset: *MONA also offers double decker open top bus tours of neon signs in Hollywood. Photos courtesy of MONA museum*

One of the museum's most popular events is the evening Neon Cruise, which shows Los Angeles in a whole new light. An open-top double decker bus cruises past classic movie marquees, Chinatown's glowing pagodas, and all that glitters in Hollywood.

It's a great way for tourists to learn the history of Los Angeles, according to Siegel.

Housed in a former mansion in the neighborhood, the Brand Library and Art Center focuses on visual arts and music, with a schedule of concerts, lectures, dance performances, and hands-on crafts.

TROLLING

Why is the new Bay Bridge safer?

Every time you cross the Bay Bridge there are eyes on you. It's not a villain in an Alfred Hitchcock movie, but rather a tiny hero, a steel troll perhaps 18 inches tall, who hides out in the dark recesses and makes sure the bridge is safe.

He's not the first troll to call the bridge home. In 1989 the Loma Prieta earthquake caused the top section of the bridge to collapse. Michael Bondi's blacksmith shop was hired for ironwork, and he thought it was a good opportunity to attach a gargoyle. Instead, his employee Bill Roan suggested a troll resembling Billy Goat Gruff who would live under the bridge and keep it safe. The idea was nixed by the state transportation commission, and yet this scary mythological creature with large horns, carrying a wrench, magically appeared attached to the last section of the bridge.

It was a secret until a reporter discovered the troll, and then the whole world knew about it, says Bart Nye, public information officer for the Bay Bridge.

Although the troll did a good job keeping the bridge safe for more than a decade, seismic experts later recommended replacing the entire eastern span. American Steel was hired for the job, and the builders asked Bondi and his team to create another troll.

GUARDIAN OF MOTORISTS

WHAT: Bay Bridge troll

WHERE: Your guess is as good as mine.

COST: Free unless you rent a boat to try and spot it.

PRO TIP: For the first time since the Bay Bridge was built in 1933, you can now walk or bike across the eastern span.

Left: *Skippers sail under the Bay Bridge in hopes of spotting the troll.*

Right: *Bill Roan and Michael Bondi show off their lucky troll. Photo courtesy of Michael Bondi*

Inset: *Bart Nye says hi to an old friend. Photo courtesy of Bart Nye, PIO Bay Bridge*

"You can't see it from the roadway due to safety, but the troll is out there protecting drivers," says Nye. "If you get lucky with binoculars you might see him, but it takes away from the fun to reveal where it is. Trolls like to hide."

From dusk to dawn you can see 25,000 white LED lights on the Bay Bridge, but only if you're not driving! This permanent art installation is positioned so motorists won't be distracted.

WATERWAYS

What do Venice and San Francisco have in common?

There are lots of transportation options along San Francisco's Embarcadero: the trolley, pedi cabs, buses, and rideshares. But the least known is the most scenic.

The San Francisco Water Taxi takes passengers from the Ferry Building to Pier 39 and Fisherman's Wharf for only $10. "Cheapest way to get on the water," says owner Dave Thomas, who claims the prices have not gone up since 1928—the last time there was a water taxi. "It was very expensive back then." Now, he says, it has been listed as one of the best cheap dates.

Thomas says you never know what will happen during your ride. Once a rider whispered to the captain that they wanted to scatter a beloved's ashes. The captain suggested asking the other passengers if it was OK. They said, "Yes, we have a problem, we want to sing." Turns out they were members of a gospel choir, and they sang "Amazing Grace." "It was one of those magical moments that can only happen on water," says Thomas. Another ash scattering was not as idyllic—the wind changed, and the ashes came back and hit the captain in the face!

Marriage proposals, which are popular on the water taxi, can also go wrong. Once a young man proposed and she said no. "It was an awkward trip back to shore. Talk about chilly," chuckles Thomas.

After visiting the farmers' market in the Ferry Building on Saturday morning, take the water taxi to the Hyde Street Pier and walk along Fisherman's Wharf and the Aquatic Park beach.

Left: *The Water Taxi has some of the best views of San Francisco.*

Right: *The Water Taxi stops at Pier 39 where you can watch the frolicking sea lions.*

FRISCO FLOAT

WHAT: San Francisco Water Taxi

WHERE: Pier 1.5, Pier 39

COST: $10

PRO TIP: You can also book the Water Taxi for private events.

Skippers, many of them women, will point out historic sites such as Fisherman's Wharf, Pier 39, the Ferry Building, the Exploratorium, the ballpark, Mission Bay, and Chase Center. The ferry typically leaves on the hour, but the schedule depends on the weather.

Just look for the yellow and black checkered signs or a skipper holding a water taxi sign. By the way, they all know where the nearest bathrooms are before and after the trip and they only take cash.

SLAPSTICK WINE

What wine pairs best with rubber chicken?

When you mention wine country, Napa comes to mind, but more and more people are discovering the intimate tasting experience in the Gold Country. Maybe it's living in "mountain time," as locals call it, but in Murphy's they're just more relaxed.

Take the Twisted Oak Winery. While Napa wine snobs extol the qualities of a wine, ranging from acidic to zippy, Twisted Oak owner Jeff "El Jefe" Stai muses about rubber chickens. Stai explains, "We bottled our first three wines back in 2003, and I was having trouble coming up with words for the back label that weren't insufferable like most back labels. Finally I was sitting with friends having some wine when I saw my old rubber chicken hanging on the wall, and there it was: 'Enjoy this wine with a bunch of friends and a rubber chicken.'

The day the winery opened, the first customer bought a whole case and as he paid for it asked where's the rubber chicken? "I didn't have an answer, but I clearly needed one!" Stai says. "So I hit the internet looking for a good source and started buying them by the gross." Now plastic poultry adorns the store and the vineyard.

To reach the vineyard, visitors drive over rolling green hills dotted with cows until they reach a gravel path with these unusual directional signs: "Rubber Chickens Have Right of

---

Nearby Moaning Caverns is the largest cave chamber in California, tall enough to hold the Statue of Liberty! An old mining shaft, it got its name from the cave's moaning sounds. Gold miners lowered themselves by rope, but you can walk the staircase or try zip lining.

Left: *The rubber chicken national forest is on the way to the Twisted Oak Winery.*

Right: *Twisted Oak is located in the Gold Country's rolling hills.*

Inset: *Look out for the rubber chickens— they're everywhere.*

LAIDBACK LIBATIONS OR WINE TASTING WITHOUT THE ATTITUDE

WHAT: Twisted Oak Winery

WHERE: 4280 Red Hill Rd., Vallecito

COST: $10 for tastings

PRO TIP: If you can't bear to leave the chickens, you can camp overnight in your self-contained RV for free. Reserve through harvesthosts.com.

Way" and "No Clucking Zone." This is leading up to the Rubber Chicken National Forest, where bright yellow rubber poultry hangs from oak trees.

Twisted Oak also offers underground tours of its caves, which are the size of a football field. You might see stalactites, but you will definitely taste wine directly from the barrels. There is also a Twisted Oak tasting room in downtown Murphy's at 363 Main Street.

WOODEN ACTORS

Who's pulling the strings in Hollywood?

"Puppets are having a renaissance," says Missy Steele, operations manager for the Bob Baker Marionette Theater in Los Angeles. Previously shunned, wooden actors are now in demand thanks to shows like Showtime's *Kidding*, Michelle Obama's Netflix show *Waffles + Mochi*, and *Earth to Ned* on Disney. The Screen Actors Guild recently took the unusual step of recognizing puppeteers as actors with a special skill.

Before streaming services discovered marionettes, LA native Bob Baker was a fan. After seeing a puppet show as a child, he created a petite theater in his backyard and soon became the modern-day Geppetto. Over his lifetime he handcrafted 3,000 puppets that performed in the Bob Baker Marionette Theater, the longest-running puppet theater in the United States.

He pioneered theater in the round, "a cabaret style of artistry where puppets may sit in your lap and engage you in conversation," says Steele. You see the artists pulling the strings, but you quickly forget about them as the marionettes come to life.

MERRY MARIONETTES

WHAT: Bob Baker Marionette Theater

WHERE: 4949 York Blvd., Los Angeles

COST: Varies

PRO TIP: Buy tickets in advance because they're often sold out.

After the show, treat the kids to sarsaparilla at Galco's Soda Pop Stop. This Italian grocery has over 600 varieties of soda, with unusual flavors such as dandelion, cucumber, birch, and tamarind!

Top left: *The Bob Baker Marionette Theater has an old-fashioned marquee.*

Top right: *Is it time to entertain yet?*

Left inset: *Clowning around is part of the job here.*

Center inset: *The audience is so engrossed in the music and the characters they forget a human is pulling the puppet's strings.*

Right inset: *It's tough to pick a favorite puppet, there are so many adorable characters.*

When Baker died at 90, the theater shuttered, but his staff found another location in 2019: a former vaudeville auditorium. "We have a lot of celebrity friends who do appearances at special events, so you never know who you might see!," teases Steele.

Perhaps a famous Disney character! Baker also worked for Walt Disney; his Disneyland window displays are legendary, and he was given exclusive rights to create puppets of select Disney characters.

ALL ABOARD

Why are rail cars sitting in the middle of a field?

Train buffs are in luck. BART (Bay Area Rapid Transit) is looking for new homes for old train cars. Prospective parents can adopt a car and repurpose it as a brewpub, art installation, quirky store, or park it on their farm. If you have enough space, you can turn it into a workshop, guest house, man cave, or she shed.

Those who want to adopt have to pass a screening process: they must use the cars for positive purposes and develop a "retirement" plan. In other words, the cars must be recycled, not dumped in the ocean (fish don't care for aluminum) or left on the side of the road. "If you want to take it to Burning Man that's fine, but you can't leave it in the desert," says Alicia Trost, BART's chief communications officer.

The key caveat: you're responsible for moving the car from the BART yard to your location, and renting a flatbed truck and crane will cost around $10,000, says Trost.

ENDLESS COMMUTE

WHAT: BART car giveaway

WHERE: Unusual places all over the Bay Area

COST: No need for a Clipper card to board, price varies

PRO TIP: If you can't afford a BART car, don't despair. BART is considering selling pieces of its history online.

One of the most interesting BART stops is Orinda. It's walking distance to the Orinda Theatre, an Art Deco movie palace in the Streamline Moderne style.

Top left: *If you liked your commute why not take Bart home with you? Bart's auctioning off older cars to free up room in the warehouse for new trains. Photo courtesy of BART*

Top right: *You can walk to the historic Orinda Theater from the BART station. Photo courtesy of Derek Zemrak*

Bottom left: *Bart's funky citron yellow and aqua blue seats are back in style! Photo courtesy of John Williamson*

Bottom right: *BART takes passengers to hidden treasures like the Orinda Theater.*

What do people do with these 40-year-old relics? BART has received interest from movie producers, sports teams, Airbnb owners, railroad museums, and fire departments who use them as training tools. Antique cars in other cities have found new uses as emergency shelters after major disasters and as housing for the homeless.

BART, which originated in 1973, says if the 600 retired cars are not adopted, they'll be shredded and recycled.

CARDIFF CRACK

Where can you enjoy crack without being arrested?

Residents of Cardiff by the Sea and Ireland have something in common . . . they often ask if you're up for a bit of crack. In both cases, say yes! In Ireland, crack, spelled craic, means fun while in this small California beach town it means having fun while eating meat. Not just any meat . . . Burgundy Pepper tri tip from Seaside Market. It's so addictive customers nicknamed it Cardiff Crack.

In the late 1980's the owners, John and Pete Najjar, wanted to create an affordable meal for campers swarming to Elijo state campground every year, so they experimented with various spices and developed a secret process to infuse the beef with marinade. Over the years it developed a cult following with fans forming lines outside the door around Christmas.

HOOKED ON TRI TIP

WHAT: Seaside Market

WHERE: 2087 San Elijo Avenue, Cardiff by the Sea

COST: Varies, currently $12.00 a pound

PRO TIP: It's the perfect treat to enjoy on the beach located across the street.

Another eccentric attraction in Encinitas are the huge boat houses at 726 Third Street. When the Moonlight Dance Hall and Bathhouse went dark, architect Miles Kellogg used the reclaimed wood to build the SS *Moonlight* and the SS *Encinitas*, which resemble sea faring vessels but have always been in dry dock.

Top left: *Locals know this is THE place for tri-tip.*

Top right: *Cross the street to enjoy tri-tip on the beach.*

Bottom left: *Cardiff by the Sea is a laid-back beach town that enjoys barbeques.*

Bottom right: *Cardiff crack is world famous.*

The warm weather here means barbecues are almost a daily occurrence and if locals want to impress, they serve Cardiff Crack. "Grilling Crack gives grillers instant street cred," says local Andy Robinson. "You can completely butcher the stuff, and the seasoning is so good people will still think you're some kind of genius behind the Weber." His wife Carrie adds, "It's just fun ordering 'crack' at the meat counter and nobody gets arrested."

Resident Shelley Kilburn says ask any San Diegan if they want some crack and they instinctively know what you're talking about. "Who knew such an ordinary cut of meat could be so addictive, but it is called Crack, after all." Word of the tri tip has spread, and it's shipped to customers in Hawaii, the East Coast, and Alaska.

SOURCES

A Many-sided Story: Site visit, nscda-ca.org, sfhistory.org

All Aboard: Site visit, interview with Alicia Trost, BART, chief communications officer

Art House: Site visit, 500cappstreet.org, artistshomes.org, savingplaces.org

Baker Street West: Site visit, interview with Linda Hein aka Mrs. Hudson, Bakerstreetwest.com

Beachware: Site visit, El Cerrito historical society, Richmond Museum of History & Culture, richmondmuseum.org

Blessed Beach: Site visit, interview with Lauren Landress, Director of Public Affairs, Self-Realization Fellowship, yogananda.org

Bolinas Bubble: Site visit, UCSF study: ucsf.edu/news/2020/06/417791/town-bolinas-antibody-tests-find-minimal-history-infection

Born in a Barn: Site visit, interview Maggie Christie, hollywoodheritage.org, paramountstudios.com

Cardiff Crack: Site Visit, interview with Pete Najjar, V.P. Seaside Market, seasidemarket.com

Carmelot: Site visits, interview with Sandra Book, director of tourism, Carmel-by-the-Sea, Carmelchamber.org, Torhouse.org

Cheese War: Site visits, visitpacifica.com, interview with Kathleen Manning, Pacifica Historical Society, pacificahistory.org, Nicksrestaurant.net

Chicken Boy: Site visit, interview Annie Inoyue, chickenboy.com

Circus Cemetery: Site visit, interview with Marta Quinn, Showfolks of America

City Camping: Interview with Aricia Martinez, Presidio Visitor Services, presidio.gov

Crafty church: Site visit, interview with Reverend Junchol Lee, Swedenborgian Church, sfswedenborgian.org

Dangerous Paintings: Site visit, *On the Edge of America*, Chapter 4, Politics and Modernism: The Trial of the Rincon Annex Murals by Gray Brechin

Dive Bar Dioramas Site visit, interview artist Michael E. Long, michaelevanlong.com

Dog and Cat Show: Site visit, interview with John Natsoulas, natsoulas.com

Doo Doo Dilmena: Site visit, KQED.org

Eggheads: Site visit, interviews with Karen Nikos-Rose, UC Davis public relations, Sandra Shannonhouse, Trustee Robert Arneson Trust, ucdavis.edu

Eternal Hollywood: Site visit, interview with Kari Bible, cemetarytour.com, Hollywoodforever.com

Famous Frogs: Site visit, interviews with Sandie Lema, Frogtown public relations

Fast Food Fantasy: Site visit, visitpacifica.com, sfrecpark.org, pacifica-land-trust.org, visitcalifornia.com

Felicitations: Site visit, interview with Jacques-André Istel, founder Felicity, CA

Freaks and Geeks Welcome: Site visit, interview with Carl Crew

Frisco Frivolity: Site visits, interviews with Peter Kasin, Natonal Park Service, nps.gov

From Russia with Love: Site Visits, interview with Teri Davena, office of Economic Development, Benecia, Visitbenecia.org, nps.gov

Fuschia Fun: Site visit, Madonnainn.com, interview with Thomas Kessler, , Exec. Dir., History Center San Luis Obispo County, historycenterslo.org

Gallery of Gardens: Site visit, interview with Benjamin Godfrey, landscape manager, Cornerstone Sonoma, CornerstoneSonoma.com

Going Batty: Interview with Corky Quirk, yolobasin.org

Hand of the Land: Site visit, interview with Gordon Huether, gordonhuether.com, napaartwalk.org, ciaatcopia.com

Harp (Speak) Boontling: Interview with Wes Smith, Anderson Valley Historical Society, Anderson Valley Brewing Company

Heaven Can Wait: Site visit, Susan O'Sullivan, public relations, Filoli

Hollywood North: Interview with Rena Azevedo Kiehn, public relations, Niles Essanay Silent Film Museum, book-Bronco Billy and the Essanay Film Company, Nilesfilmmuseum.org, museumoflocalhistory.org

Hot Museum: Site visit, interview with James J. Lee, Trustee Chair, Guardians of the City, guardiansofthecity.org

Hurray for Hollywood: Site visit, thehollywoodroosevelt.com

Indulge in Illusion: Site visit, interview with Gerry Griffin, gerrygriffinmagic.com

It's Complicated: Site visit, interview with Jennifer George, Goldberg's grandaughter, Rube Goldberg Institute for Innovation & Creativity, rubegoldberg.com

Liquid Gold: Site visit, interview with Conrad Levasseur, ironstonevineyards.com, gocalaveras.com

Mannequin Madness: Site visit, interview with Judi Townsend, mannequinmadness.com

Marina Moods: Site visit, interview with Art Scampa

Metamorphosis: Site Visits, interview with Gregangelo Herrera, gregangelomuseum.com

Mod Mediterrean: Site visit, interview with Jeff Shelton, jeffsheltonarchitect.com/santa-barbara-map

Motel Milestone: Site visit, interview with Thomas Kessler, SLO museum

Museum in Motion: Site visit, interview with Rick Laubscher, President and Ceo, Market St. Railway, streetcar.org

Mystery Spot: Site visit, mysteryspot.com

Natural Art: Site visits, presidio.gov

Our Lady of Touchdowns: Site visit, interview with Rosemary Alva, author of Our Lady's Way

Paper Treasures: Site visit, Karpeles.com

Pig Palace: Site visit, interviews with Laurie Armstrong, public relations and Matt Leffert, Executive Director, Jack London State Historic Park. jacklondonpark.com

Pool Party: Interview with Liz Dugan, annenbergbeachhouse.com

Precious Park: Site visit, interview with Steve Staiger, Palo Alto Historical Association, Darren Anderson Assistant Director Open Space, City of Palo Alto, , Steve Staiger, Palo Alto Historical Association, cityofpaloalto.org

Presidential Penthouse: Sources: Site visit, interview with Michelle Heston, Fairmont public relations

Propaganda Power: Site visit, interview with Tom Areton, museumofpropaganda.org

Rancho Shazam: Site visit, interview with Lee Greenberg, founder Rancho Shazam.

Regal Rolls: Site visit, interview with Chris Trenschel, President, Santa Barbara Lawn Bowls Club, santabarbaralbc.org, worldbowls.com, quinlanmuseum.com, santabarbaralbc.org

Researching Big Foot: Interview with Michael Rugg, curator, Bigfoot Discovery Museum, bigfootdiscoveryproject.com, santacruz.org

Ribbit: Site visit, edhat.com

Robolights: Site visit, interview with Kenny Irwin, Kennyirwinartist.com

Rock Star: site visit, interview with Dave Dean, Dave's Rock Garden

Roman Holiday: Site visit, interview with Annie Morhauser, Annieglass.com, Taylorreinhold.com, city of Watsonville.org

Sacramento's Second City: Site visit, interview with Delta Pick Mello, executive director and CEO, Sacramento History Museum, sachistorymuseum.org

Sand Castle: Site visit, interview with Jeannette Cool, executive director Sam Mazza foundation, visitpacifica.com

Sassy Swine: Site visit, interview with name she prefers:"Pig House Lady"

Scandinavian Style: site visit, "The Church by the Golden Gate" by Dagfinn Kvale

Scentsiblity: Site visit, interview with Mandy Aftel, Aftelier.com

Seeing Red: Site visit, mrcsf.org, interviews, Russiancentersf.com

SF's Secret Weapon: Site Visit, interview with Jennifer Gilbert, thealbioncastle.com

Shady Business: Site visit,tours@ undergroundgardens.com

Slapstick Wine: Site visit, interview with Jeff Stai, owner Twisted Oak winery, twistedoak.com

Stagecoach Stop: Site visit, interview with Paris Trefz General Manager Cold Spring Tavern, coldspringstavern.com

Surf Art: Site visit, interview with Catherine Blakespear, mayor Encinitas, encintasvisitorscenter.com

Suspenseful San Diego: Site visit, sandiego.org, sandiegohistory.org

Tacky Titans: Site visit, interview with Bruce Kennedy, owner Bell Plastics, bellplasticsfabrication.com

Thornburg village: Site visit, Berkekleyheritage.com

Toad tunnel: Site Visit, interview with Bob Bowen, retired city of Davis spokesperson, UCdavis.edu, cityofdavis.org

Trolling: Site visit, interviews with Michael Bondi, Bart Nye, PIO, Bay Bridge, museumca.org

Truth Seekers Sanctuary: Site visit, interview with Kelly Carmen, prs.org

Utopia in Tiburon: site visit, interview with David M. Gotz, Archivist, Belvedere-Tiburon Landmarks Society, landmarkssociety.com

Walk like an Egyptian: site visit, interview with Julie Scott, executive director, egyptianmuseum.org,

Water Worship: SF Public Utilities Commission, sfpuc.org

Waterways: Site visit, interview with Dave Thomas, owner the San Francisco Water Taxi, sanfranciscowatertaxi.org

What a Gas!: Interview with Corrie Siegel, executive director, MONA, neonmona.org

Wild West: Site visit, interview with Suzanne Statler, co-founder Port Costa museum, warehousecafeportcosta.com

Wooden Actors: Site visit, interviews with Alex Evans, executive director and head puppetter and Missy Steele, operations manager, Bob Baker Marionette Theater, bobbakermarionettetheater.com

ZZYZX: Dr. Anne Kelly, Program Director, Research and Education, CSU Desert Studies Center, nps.gov

INDEX

199